Software Asset Management

Understanding and Implementing an optimal solution

PRAFULL VERMA and
KALYAN KUMAR

Trademark acknowledgement

In addition to the registered trademarks, many of the designations are used by product vendors and other organizations to distinguish their products and services and may be claimed as the trademarks or service marks. Authors acknowledge such designations and used those designations including trademarks, in initial caps or all caps.

ISBN: 0692324267
ISBN 13: 9780692324264

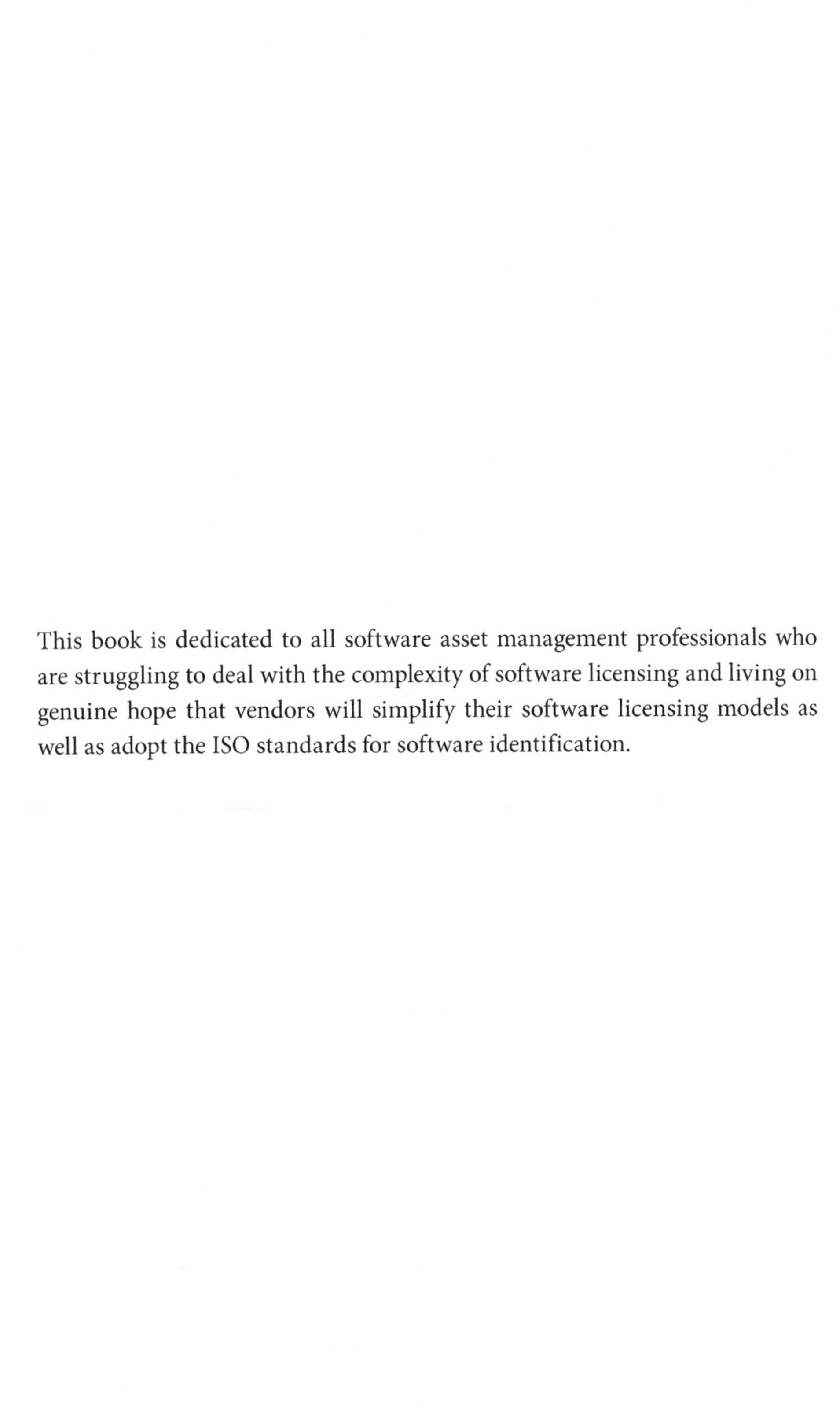

This book is dedicated to all software asset management professionals who are struggling to deal with the complexity of software licensing and living on genuine hope that vendors will simplify their software licensing models as well as adopt the ISO standards for software identification.

ACKNOWLEDGMENTS

We did not have any plan to publish a book on this subject, but the idea of publishing crystallized during our work of starting a practice and developing a standard solution and best practice to address the emerging complexities in the current market.

Originally it started with a white paper about an optimal solution. During our regular professional work, we also conducted a few workshops. The discussions during the workshop led into details. The workshops created a need for education as well. When we incorporated all the educative points and our points of view on this subject, the white paper became this book.

We want to sincerely thank people who asked questions on this topic and debated and inspired us to spell out our views and opinions. We want to especially thank customers whom we serve and who need to be educated that SAM is much beyond a tool game.

Within our organization we had encouragement and support to pursue our passion of sharing our knowledge and experience. The very first name on our list is C. Vijaykumar. We have acknowledged in the past as well that his vision and enablement have helped us to fruition our earlier publications. Anytime and every time we have an opportunity like this, we will continue to acknowledge his direct and indirect support and reiterate our thanks.

And finally, we both thank our individual family members—Annie and Naomi; Zulfia and Azlan—who kept us motivated during this period.

Prafull Verma
Kalyan Kumar

FOREWORD

No one imagined software would become an asset someday and would be managed like other asset classes. But in this age, software is becoming an important asset, and a software portfolio has to be managed efficiently like any other class of asset.

However, software, and resulting applications, is a complex asset to manage. It has several layers that could have different ownerships, different life cycles, and different costing or pricing models. Operating systems, databases, and application servers are layers that lie underneath almost all custom-created applications. Even in the case of packaged software like ERPs (enterprise resource planning), usually the operating system and database can be chosen by the customer. Thus licensing of software is a major aspect of asset management, as each layer, each component, and the package as a whole have to be dealt with as a combined unit for some purposes and as separate entities for some other purposes like accounting or renewal.

Modern-day enterprises have thousands of software applications, or assets, that are deployed across different parts of the world. Managing the licenses that lie underneath all these applications is a mammoth task by itself. Steep annual maintenance charges (AMCs) to the order of 20% of the listed cost, or sometimes even more, are a major part of the "run" cost of IT. Headaches associated with an out-of-support software layer resulting in forced upgrades are routine matters now. Licensing terms and conditions heavily favor big software makers that rule the world in ERPs, operating systems, e-mails, databases, and so forth. Large corporations of today have such a heavy dependence on software that business virtually runs on software. Software makers are aware of this dependence and exploit it well to their advantage by unilaterally raising the AMCs or changing terms and conditions of usage, which at times can make previously compliant software require additional licenses. A friendly sales guy from the software vendors informs you someday that you are out of compliance and that there is a considerable risk associated with it that you never realized before. The terms and conditions that you sign while procuring software often include clauses that give access to the software vendors to conduct audits to verify that you have the right number of licenses, which is somewhat unnerving as invariably they find some excess usage over and above the licensed ones. For large corporations that have thousands of third-party software licenses across the world with a dynamic workforce comprising employees, contractors, and outsourced vendors, some extra usage or remnant licenses do creep into the system. But software vendors put in such one-sided terms and conditions that none of these are taken into consideration, and steep penalties are enforced in the form of agreeing to buy some enterprise licenses, site licenses, or the latest hardware that will subsume some licenses or agreeing to replace some competing product—say e-mail by their own e-mail software, for example. The legal threat from the software vendors is taken seriously as it could stop the very functioning of the business; thus companies are made to cough up this money and again sign on the dotted line with similar terms and conditions that will exploit them in the future without fail. So this whole licensing game and the audit façade is well planned, well orchestrated, and "by design," not by accident.

Perhaps it would serve some purpose to take a look at how we landed in this situation and how software engineering was born some five decades back. At that time, scientists related to defense systems and aeronautics working in places like NASA or JPL were prolific writers of software code in earlier-generation languages like FORTRAN or assembly language or machine language depending upon resource constraints like memory, which was very precious those days. Having four kilobytes of onboard memory on a spacecraft was like a dream. Programmers in those days used all kinds of techniques like self-modifying code and highly "goto"-oriented code to reuse every byte of memory in a very ingenious manner. The programmer who wrote the code would invariably run and maintain it for its lifetime, so one was free to choose the most complex but most compact way of writing great code. Programmers were proud of their complex code that achieved highly complex, real-time, and intelligent tasks in those days. In about 1980 or so, structured programming and newer programming languages came about that gave huge importance to a very systematic way of writing code and never using goto-like constructs, and great emphasis was given to maintainability of code as it dawned on people who were writing code for commercial applications using languages like Cobol that the writer and maintainer of software need not be the same person. This was a very important departure, which perhaps led to the creation of the entire software industry since maintenance could be done by someone else (someone probably less gifted); hence, ideas related to outsourcing must have occurred somewhere down the line. But in this process, we whipped programmers who wrote complex code and instead insisted that code be written as simply as possible, be well documented, and be well tested with all test cases also documented, and so forth—all good things for an industry to take birth, but at the cost of dumbing down the whole programming community to a good extent. Now, once you start dumbing down, you can't stop at a particular point. The whole education and training associated with software engineering also produced millions of ordinary programmers or software engineers who could maintain someone else's code most of the time. So, a lot that this book addresses has roots in the fundamental way in which the art and science of programming, almost bordering to religion, was transformed into an industry where factory models were preferred for code writing as well as maintaining. Somehow the greatness of some of the original programmers of yesteryears is still leveraged or exploited by the industry as an image booster or for branding.

I sincerely hope Prafull and Kalyan's book address some of these aspects and makes the end-user companies, and software users in general, more prudent in their decision to buy software and, more importantly, to inspect the license agreements carefully and negotiate before signing on the dotted line. We spend a huge deal of time and energy in negotiating the license cost but hardly spend 5% of time in carefully reviewing the licensing terms and conditions. Perhaps it should be the other way around. Perhaps the book will also provide ideas around open-source software and whether it can liberate us from the tyranny of licensed software by big vendors. Obviously there is no single answer, and every company has to weigh several options based on its context and its industry. But hopefully this book will help us question our own thinking process about handing software as an asset.

Kavindra Sharma
Global Head, Consulting Services
L & T Infotech

TABLE OF CONTENT

1 INTRODUCTION TO SAM

Software asset management (SAM), in its current form, is a relatively new discipline in the IT industry. In the good old days, the software was supplied as a part of hardware by the same vendor, and there was no need for tracking software. As the open-system movement grew and independent software and application vendors entered in the market, the need arose for license accounting. The tracking of hardware and software was delinked. License accounting was still very simple until 1990 because of simple license models and a limited number of products. Shrink-wrapped software was sold and tracked like hardware items from an asset-management perspective. Complexity grew rapidly because of multiple reasons—the increased complexity of licensing models, the multiplication of software products, and the lack of standards on making software identifiable. The legal-compliance requirements and the associated costs forced industry to address the software license-management problems, and a formal discipline emerged. It also led to an emerging pricing model where the value of the software was based on what the purchaser could afford or the perceived value outcome of the license and not on the actual ground-up cost of building and maintaining the software.

Now we can say that a general consensus about the definition of SAM is established—software asset management is the practice of using people, processes, and technology to systematically track, evaluate, and manage software licenses and their usage. According to ITIL (Information Technology

Infrastructure Library), software asset management book ISBN 978-0-11-330943-6 it includes "all of the infrastructure and processes necessary for the effective management, control, and protection of the software assets within an organization, throughout all stages of their lifecycle." The role of software asset management in an organization is to reduce IT costs and limit business and legal risk related to the ownership and use of software while maximizing IT responsiveness and end-user productivity.

Like all our other books, the purpose of this book is to educate and provide guidance in the subject area. SAM should be considered as a mainstream service-management discipline. In most organizations, it is limited to a license-accounting function using Excel sheets and discovery tools. In more mature IT organizations, SAM is very well recognized and established as a mainstream service discipline. Our observation is that even in these mature organizations, SAM is largely a tool-driven work. No doubt the tools are absolutely essential, but the nontechnology parts of SAM are no less important. We want to present a direction for SAM solution that is architecture driven. The target audiences of this book are IT generalist and SAM functional consultants.

SAM versus License Management

SAM is a comprehensive discipline, as we learn from the definition. As you go further in this book, you will learn that it is a set of multiple processes, tools and functions, and governance. License management is a limited part within SAM. In fact, license management is the logical start for any SAM program and focuses on knowing what you have deployed and what you have purchased and reconciling one against the other.

Asset versus License

A license is the right to use the software. A software license has economic value—therefore, it is considered as an asset—while the installed instance of the software may be a CI (configuration item). Asset is thus the right to use and not the intellectual property associated with the software. Rather than being an asset, software for use could create a liability if not properly licensed."

Hardware-Asset Management versus SAM

Hardware-asset management can be well done around asset database, and CMDB (configuration management database) is not required. (In our other book,-process excellence for IT operations- we discussed asset DB versus CMDB.) The cost and value of hardware is independent of the software installed on it or its status. For example, a sever costs you $xx regardless of whether it is in production or in stock and also regardless of whether it is running a database or some other application. On the other hand, the value of the software may depend on the hardware on which it runs. (You pay more for running software on a quad-core CPU than running it on a dual-core CPU.) Therefore, it is impossible to manage software assets without also managing the hardware on which the software runs, and the hardware-asset management becomes an integral part of SAM as well as a prerequisite for SAM. Most of the SAM components (process, function, and tools) can be used for hardware-asset management also.

Executable versus Nonexecutable Software

SAM scope is perceived to be only for executable software such as operating systems, utilities, and application programs, but SAM principles can be used for all software, regardless of the nature of the software, including nonexecutable software (such as fonts, graphics, audio and video recordings, templates, dictionaries, documents, and data).

Copyright violations are most often related to nonexecutable software. And most often these violations occur due to the lack of knowledge and awareness.

One very common example is the birthday greeting song. Do you know that the most popular and most played song of the world, "Happy Birthday to You," is copyrighted by the publishing arm of Warner Music Group?

This does not mean that everyone who sings or plays "Happy Birthday to You" to family members at birthday parties without obtaining the prior permission or paying the royalty is involved in copyright infringement, because the permission or the royalty is applicable for commercial uses of the song, such as playing or singing it for profit or using it for public performance—defined by copyright law as performances that occur at a place open to the public, or at any place where a substantial number of persons outside of a normal circle of a family and its social acquaintances is gathered. So singing or playing "Happy Birthday to You" to family members and friends at home is fine, but performing a copyrighted work in a public setting such as a restaurant technically requires a license. In real life you will rarely face prosecution for greeting a family member in a restaurant in this way.

Similarly, in enterprise, there are numerous potential violations that are so trivial that it is practical to relax the application of SAM processes and policies for them. You should, however, be very judicious in deciding what you want to focus on and to what extent.

1.1 Multidimensional Complexity

Software Product

A software product is what you buy. A product defines an overall scope, a set of functions for a specific business need. A software product, executable or nonexecutable, has intellectual property associated with it. A license agreement defines three aspects—the license agreement, the license model, and the license metrics. Each of these three aspects is individually very complex to understand. When the management of these three aspects is combined, the complexity increases multifold.

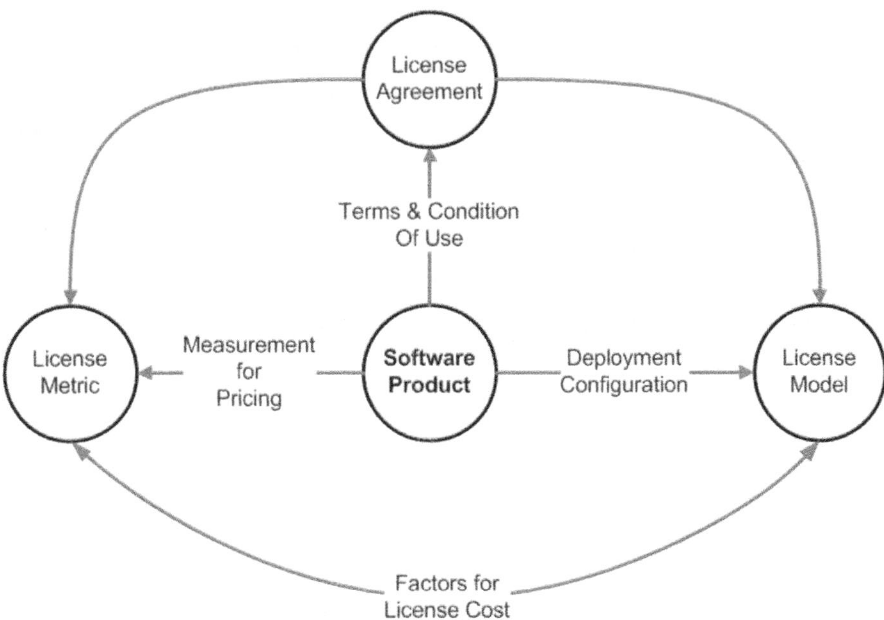

Figure 1. Multidimensional complexity

License agreement is a contract between a software company and the user of that software. The software license grants the user specific rights to use the software in specified ways. Typical T&C (terms and conditions) include legal aspects of intellectual-property (IP) protection, copyright protection, and restricting the use beyond a certain purpose. Downgrade rights, upgrade rights, transfer rights, and such matters are very common elements of license agreements. In the software industry, the most common ways of granting licenses are through a written and signed agreement or via a written shrink-wrap or click-wrap agreement, in which the user indicates acceptance of the rights and limitations in the license by opening the software package or clicking a button on a computer screen.

License model is the method of deployment or the configuration of deployment of the product—for example, if it is deployed on a single-processor machine or on a multiprocessor machine or on a cluster. Different models usually have different license metrics.

License metric defines the measurement of usage for the pricing calculation. A license metric determines how the software usage is being measured when the license granter grants the license—for example, measurement on a per-user basis or a per-processor basis.

Frequently the combined aspect that includes the deployment configuration and the measurement metrics is termed as the license model. In other words, the license model is deemed as the license model plus the license metric.

1.1.1 License Genre

The license genres given here are popular and common terms in circulation about the license classes. Each license type here, by definition, is a mix of a license model and terms and conditions and sometimes the metric as well. People are familiar with movie genres and literary genres. These refer to the theme or topic or issues or concepts that the film or the literature revolves around. A movie can fall into more than one genre—for example, romantic comedy. Similarly, license genre is the theme of license model, metric, and agreement under which the license is granted. A license can have more than one genre. The apt example in this case is licenses that are used for a specific purpose or specific business model, like outsourcing/managed service provider.

Beta-Test License

Beta-test agreement is a software license agreement between a software developer and a user that allows the user to use the software program in a live environment ahead of releasing it to the general public. Beta-test agreements differ from general-purpose commercial software licenses. They typically have more significant limitations on liability, provide very limited warranties or no warranty, and may require user evaluation and feedback. This is also known as a software beta-test agreement. Beta licenses are usually free of cost as the software may not be of production grade.

Capacity or Performance

A licensing model based on the host computer's (one or more servers) capacity or performance can be used for compute-intensive applications such as databases or transaction processing. For example, for IBM software, licensees can use full-capacity licensing or virtualization capacity (subcapacity) licensing. If using full-capacity licensing, the licensee must obtain PVU (processor value unit) entitlements sufficient to cover all activated processor cores in the physical hardware environment made available to or managed by the program, except for those servers from which the program has been permanently removed. If using virtualization capacity licensing, the licensee must obtain entitlements sufficient to cover all activated processor cores made available to or managed by the program, as defined according to the virtualization capacity license counting rules.

Cross License

This is the licensing agreement between two software manufacturers and not with the customer or end user. Cross licenses are granted by a patent holder to another patent holder—may be a competitor—who reciprocates with a similar license, which is designed to control the marketing of the products involved or to further their development for larger market segment. This is a method of exchanging the rights, usually on a no-cash basis. This kind of license will not be in the scope of enterprise SAM.

Development License

You do not need to buy full production licenses of the software that you will use for testing, developing, demonstration, or design of your solution or application or to create some derivative work. Microsoft's MSDN is a good example of this.

Group License

This type of license can be used to develop a consortium. It grants rights only to members of a specific group, such as named entities, those who adhere to a particular standard, or those who have received a particular certification. Group licenses may require licensees to grant special rights to all members of the group such as mandatory no-fee cross licensing.

Demo or Evaluation License

Such licenses are granted for a short time, such as thirty days or a number of uses. Usually, production-level work is not allowed, and some features may be limited or disabled, or it may have a time bomb that disables the product at a certain time. The types of users, platforms, content, or tools may also be prescribed.

Duplicate Grouping

License sharing by user, host, or display grouping defines rules for counting usage when a single user concurrently runs the same application on several computers. This instance may count as a single use or a multiple use, depending on the license terms.

Exclusive License

In exclusive licenses, the licensee is the only party to whom certain rights are granted. Such licenses are rare because they increase the licensor's opportunity cost. The rigorous limitations to exclusivity can be any combination of time, territory, industry, named competitors, exercisable features (singly, in combination, or in unrelated groups), field of use, or any of the myriads of possible business or legal terms.

Floating or Concurrent License

Concurrent license is usually applicable to multiuser systems and is based on the number of simultaneous users accessing the software. For example, in a five-user concurrent-use license, after five users are logged on to the system and accessing the software, the sixth user is prohibited. When any one of the first five log out, the next person can log in. Most often concurrent licensing can be managed by the application itself, and independent software-metering tools are not required.

Perpetual License

A perpetual license is a one-time license fee that allows continued use of the software program for as long as the customer complies with all terms of the license agreement.

Term License

A term license is for a specific, limited period of time, during which the user is allowed to access and use the software. At the end of the term, the user must stop using the software or extend the term or purchase new licenses through an agreement with the software vendor.

Subscription License

A subscription license is similar to a term license and is used typically by SaaS (Software as a service) providers who license their entire SaaS service on a defined term period, and also the management of the license compliance is typically with the service provider.

Named-User License

The user name is specified when the software is purchased or registered, and while you can install the software on multiple systems, only the named user can access the software on one system at any given time.

Named-Host License

Software is licensed for use only on one or more named computer systems. Usually, CPU serial number verification or the MAC address is used to enforce this type of license.

OEM License

OEM (original equipment manufacturer) licenses are used to allow OEMs to integrate software into their products or services and then sell the combined product. OEM licenses must grant rights such as sublicensing so that the OEM can transfer rights to its channels and customers. Payments to the licensor can include license fees; royalties per license; percentage of product revenue; and number, type, and size of accounts or users. In many cases, this bundled software is an older version of a program that is also sold on its own as a standalone product. Sometimes it is a feature-limited version of the retail software, often dubbed as a "special edition" or "limited edition." The purpose is to tempt the user to purchase the current or fully functional version of the software.

Overdraft License

Such licenses grant *N* more licenses than were purchased, giving customers a way to manage peak use without violating the license. The licensor can charge a fee for overdraft protection (insurance) as well as separate fees for each overdraft license. Advantages to licensors are flexibility, simplicity, and price locks that give predictable costs.

Packages or Bundling License

Licenses of packages grant rights to use a set of functionally dependent or independent products, or bundle. Vendors define the components of the packages or bundles in the license agreement. Such licenses allow vendors to easily customize solutions on a marketing, not engineering, level.

Package Suite

A package suite license is applied to a group of product as one bundle. Package suites restrict the concurrent sharing of a package's components. For example, no two users may concurrently use Microsoft Word and Microsoft PowerPoint. Vendors use this type of license with broad product lines as a competitive price-discounting strategy.

Pay-Per-Use License

This is a growing model due to the growing SaaS market. Fees are based on actual usage. The usage counter may be based on metrics such as CPU use or on metrics related to the nature of the application.

Site License

A site license grants rights to all valid users at a named location; it may be unlimited in number or up to a certain number. This is a cost-effective option for large customers, especially where the usage load might grow quickly or varies greatly.

Time-Limited License

Such licenses have a specific, automatic expiration date that is not automatically renewed. They are used to "force" renegotiation of license terms.

Upgrade License

Upgrade terms grant rights to use upgraded versions of the software. The customer may upgrade only *X* number of times, or the customer can only use specific upgrade versions, or the customer must upgrade within a certain time period following the release of Version X. These terms encourage the installed base to use certain versions so that the licensor may withdraw or offer special pricing for support of other versions.

Volume License

This refers to bulk quantity of licenses in one deal. This form of licensing typically applies for business, government, and educational institutions, with prices for volume licensing varying depending on the type, quantity, and applicable subscription term. A single volume license key is used when installing the software licensed.

1.1.2 Licensing Metric

A license metric is a form of measurement used by software publishers to determine how many licenses you need to buy for a particular product. Common metrics for client software are per user, per device, or per installation. Basically each user, device, or installation requires one license.

License metrics for server software are not as simple. Measurement on the server side is complex because measurement takes multiple attributes into consideration, such as virtualization, hardware capabilities, processor vendor, number of sockets, and number of cores. This results in metrics consisting of complex algorithms that depend on situational data. Well-known metrics for server software include per named user, per core, and PVU (process value unit). The central theme behind making complex measurement is to determine the value of the benefit that software is delivering and make the price proportional to the benefit.

IBM defines PVU as a unit of measure used to differentiate licensing of software on distributed processor technologies (defined by processor vendor, brand, type, and model number). IBM continues to define a processor, for purposes of PVU-based licensing, to be each processor core on a chip (socket). Each software program has a unique price per PVU.

IBM PVU Example

System and CPU	PVU per core
IBM Power6 Dual Core	120
IBM Power5 Dual Core	100
Fujitsu Sparc64 VI, VII Dual Core or Quad Core	100
Intel Itanium Dual Core	100
Sun UltraSPARC IV Dual Core	100
HP-PA RISC Dual Core	100
AMD Opteron Dual Core or Quad Core	50
Intel Xeon Dual, Quad, or Hexa Core	50
Sun UltraSPARC T1 Dual, Quad, or Hexa Core	30

1.1.3 License Agreement Terms and Conditions

Terms and conditions may have a dramatic effect on the cost. The language of T&C is also largely legal and requires very careful understanding. We are presenting some of the points that we come across that are important and have an impact on compliance and costs. The following are some examples:

Some agreements include a high watermark fee for past use where usage fees are calculated based on the maximum number of concurrent users in a defined past time period (typically monthly).

Many software and utilities that are downloadable from the Internet are free for personal use and personal devices but require license purchase on corporate machines. You as an organization need to have administrative control of each and every device that the organization owns and that is exposed to such downloads.

In almost all agreements, there is a right-to-audit clause, by which you agree and grant permission to the software owner or its representative to audit your company for compliance. If you cannot eliminate this clause, you should include the method of audit and the viable documentation requirements. You can counteroffer a voluntary audit by your auditor. Also there are special terms and conditions for licenses being used for managed services by managed service providers (MSP) or outsourcing, and these conditions can be very complex with usage of software in different situations or at different sites, one-to-one, or one-to-many licensing types. These are typically enterprise licenses, which have special terms and conditions and can sometimes lead to gray areas/zones between the licensee and licensor.

1.1.4 Intriguing Industry

The word "intriguing" comes to mind when attempting to understand the reasons for and answers to the following questions:

Is there any other industry where a company can produce and sell a defective product and then charge the customer for the repair and, on top of that, may even sue its own customer?

Is there any other industry where customers continue to purchase overpriced product features that are unnecessary and add unwanted complexity?

Is there any other industry where a customer accepts defects as the standard feature and does not demand quality? And in which producers get away with bad quality?

Is there any other industry that fixes the things that are not broken and, in the attempt to do so, breaks the things that have been working fine?

Unlike all physical entities that have aging effect, software is a mathematical logic that should never age and decay. So there should never be any need for maintenance. But there is huge money in the maintenance. The real problem is the misuse of freedom of development and ability to quickly change the software. To change the physical aspect of a physical entity, you need appreciable efforts (even if it is done by machines), as compared to edit the codes of a software and recompile. In fact in modern days, even the need of compilation is eliminated. So the development is done with the advance consideration of freedom to change. A seemingly simple change in couple of lines of code may have far reaching implications on other parts of code that is rarely well understood or well documented. So with each change more problems or bugs are introduced in the previously error-free parts of code. But programmers or developers are unable to explain this quite well to their managers or business-owners and buckle-down under pressure of deadlines. They are hardworking folks routinely burning mid-night oil on fixing stuff, but their struggle is neither appreciated not understood by their bosses who simply want to keep customer commitments.

In other words the freedom without control or freedom with temptation is the main reason of poor quality of commercial software. And most commercial software has compulsions like coming out with new releases every year or two, which exacerbates the problem further by ill-conceived features, hasty development and inadequate testing. We routinely see over-promised features being under-delivered and that too not in time. However, when we see adequate controls in the area of bespoke software in mission critical business like medical science, air traffic controls we do not see these problems. It is good to understand the importance of Moses teaching in Bible "*there is no freedom without law*" at the time of delivering the Ten Commandments.

Another intriguing fact is about being irresponsible and yet thrives in business; and we want to quote the CEO of HOB Inc., from the paid advertisement of HOB Inc. in Wall Street Journal on April 25, 2014. This was in the context of the Internet security and Heartbleed (A bug in the widely used Open SSL Internet security protocol). The CEO raised the issue of development of software by people who do not follow simple principles of development and test and do not possess the necessary basic knowledge but are available at cheap price. He questioned, as well as challenged the business model of allowing the development and usage of poor quality software. He concluded that everyone using such solution acted irresponsibly. Although that was said in the context of one specific instance of problems, but in the software industry as a whole, the defects are rarely taken seriously. The business model is to push the defective product routinely on the pretext that it is impossible to produce bug free software, which is not true.

In fact IT industry is generally more fascinated by technology rather than business purpose. We are tempted to bring in an example of current trends of promoting App Stores in the enterprise IT. App store models are perfect for consumer market scenarios where the lifespan of an application is very short – hours, days or may be in weeks and the number of applications is very large. A consumer downloads a game plays for sometime and then look for new games. While in an enterprise, the lifespan of application is long and the number of applications is limited. Besides this, the software-licensing model for enterprise application is radically different. So App store in an enterprise IT environments does not make any sense, nevertheless it still it appears in the priority or desires in many enterprise IT

1.2 Typical Organizational Scenarios

The following scenarios are typical and commonly seen in many organizations, even if they do have some level of SAM in place, and you may relate these to your own organization.

1. Guidelines for software purchase are inconsistent or missing. Usually high-value software or major-vendor software (Microsoft, Oracle, IBM, SAP, etc.) are very well controlled and go through well-managed procurement processes. Much software is purchased at the departmental level outside of these procurement processes. The liability of license-terms compliance is incurred but without a point of entry in

the tracking system. These purchases may not warrant tracking from a cost or financial perspective, but the compliance liability will warrant its tracking and managing, and therefore one must ensure that it is captured at the point of purchase itself.

2. Review of software selection is inconsistent between different departments and from site to site. This points to the lack of comprehensive enterprise standards on software products. Again, enterprise architecture groups usually focus on standard big-ticket items such as products and models from big vendors, but many auxiliary software are ignored; for example, in the area of reporting and analytics, you may have different products in use among different group. In service-management tools, the portfolio is most often very inconsistent. SAM could lead to software product portfolio optimization. Sometimes software selection is bypassed when a user obtains software outside the purchase process.

3. Software is downloaded from unauthorized locations. The Internet has made it very easy to obtain software from anywhere, anytime. Even within the enterprise, installable software of multiple versions are stored on the network without any access controls. Preventing the use of unauthorized software is one of the control elements of SAM that we discuss later under security controls. The term "DSL" refers to the definitive software library and is another part of SAM that deals with creating and maintaining the library of authorized software within the enterprise.

4. Organization lacks a consistent and efficient process for storing and distributing the authorized copy of the software. As per our general observation, storage and distribution are not centralized and are widely distributed responsibilities (read secondary work) based on geography or organization structure or functions. There are multiple problems with this. Let us, as an example, discuss server OS images and desktop/laptop OS images. Each organization creates and maintains the OS images for their standard server and desktop

models. The number of images depends upon not only the number of models but also the business needs. For example, you will have different images for OS for laptops for different kinds of uses such as for marketing departments, developers, engineering departments, and office employees. Each image will have certain utilities and bundled software that would be licensed by different vendors. Quite possible, some groups may produce and distribute the images on their own, and some images are centrally produced and distributed. The maintenance of images is among the most ignored functions of SAM. Similarly, different application groups would be updating and releasing different applications without central control of the common components and utilities. SAM, by virtue of DSL, would lead to the library of all authorized software in use and improve license management.

5. Enterprise lacks an efficient means to download software to a specific group on an at-need basis. An individual user may load the same software on multiple platforms at once, regardless of need. For example, the Acrobat editor, expensive software, may be installed on all machines in a marketing group although the requirement is only for Acrobat Reader, which is free, on several of them. In general, enterprise does not have effective means to manage software applications to meet their different license limitations and requirements.

6. Organization chooses to save costs by not renewing its enterprise agreement. If this occurs, several software will have to be tracked on a per-user basis, requiring a process not currently in place.

7. Organization lacks a dependable means to track and control some expensive software for which a limited number of licenses were purchased.

8. Organization lacks tools and processes to audit usage and compliance with contracts. For example, processes for identifying and reclaiming unused software are inconsistent...or nonexistent. In most cases the dedicated full-time functional roles are also missing.

In general, in any organization, users, departments, and sites have a wide variety of options—some well controlled and others not—for choosing, obtaining, and downloading software, making central license control difficult. License specifications vary between vendors, products, versions, and even specific contracts for the same version of a software package, and license details may be confusing. The variations in process and licenses make license management difficult. A well-established SAM that includes processes, tools, and functions is the answer.

1.3 SAM Goals

Software asset management deals with control and protection of the software assets within an organization, throughout all stages of their life cycle. The goal of SAM is to manage, control, and protect an organization's software assets, including management of the risks arising from the use of software assets, and a scalable, structured approach is needed to achieve this.

1.4 Software: Inherent Risks

All software products have IP associated with them, and IP rights are very complex to understand. Luckily, for SAM we do not need to understand the IP rights, we just need to recognize them and only understand the special characteristic of software from a SAM perspective.

Using without Buying

Organizations have volume-licensing contracts with software vendors that may allow for installation before reporting, and reporting is honor based with audit rights for the software manufacturer. In such scenarios, the liability of license is incurred without going through a procurement process but simply by installing/using software, even if done without proper authorization.

Because there are no physical requirements to purchase a license before using it, strong internal controls are required to ensure that reporting is correct.

Proof of License

Proof of license is the core of compliance. What constitutes "proof of license" can be a complex issue in itself. There are several problems in maintaining the proof of license. It is important to understand what is considered as the proof of license; there are certain misconceptions about it. For example, contrary to popular belief, the original license certificate and the original media for shrink-wrapped software purchased in retail does not establish the proof for regulatory purposes, which requires payment invoice.

Sometimes licenses may be lost physically because the user often does not recognize the importance of proof or license documentation, especially when he or she is using the software for the organization. Licenses may be lost administratively because a central unit may perform purchasing, obtaining consolidated licenses for all purchases that are administratively difficult to tie back to the ordering unit.

In certain cases licenses may be ordered via a reseller who does not have authority to grant the license on behalf of the manufacturer, and proper proof of license may not be received from a software manufacturer.

Worse still, proof of licenses for which an organization has paid may never be received from the manufacturer.

Also, in several of these cases, you may not even know that a license is missing and so will not take action to find them.

Understanding the T&C

Most of the software agreements have complex legal conditions that can be misunderstood even by people working in the area. Agreements detail the standard rights granted, ownership, restrictions, warranties, disclaimers, confidentialities, and so forth and are written for legal professionals, and IT professionals can find these difficult. Software is frequently upgraded, and license conditions can change with upgrades. Take for example Oracle T&C—Oracle Database Standard Edition can be licensed only on servers that have a maximum capacity of four sockets. If licensing by Named User Plus, the minimum is five Named User Plus licenses. Oracle Database Standard Edition, when used with Oracle Real Application Clusters, may only be licensed on a single cluster of servers supporting up to a total maximum capacity of four sockets. Effective with the release of 10g, the Oracle Database Standard Edition product includes the Real Applications Clusters database option. The Real Applications Clusters option is not included with any Standard Edition versions prior to 10g. Customers who obtain Oracle's Software Updates License & Support for the Standard Edition Database can upgrade to the 10g version of the product for the supported licenses. Also, customers must use Oracle Cluster Ready Services as the clusterware; third-party clusterware is not supported, *and* customers must use Automatic Storage Management to manage all data. Oracle Standard Edition One may only be licensed on servers that have a maximum capacity of two sockets.

Take another example of Microsoft, which makes a distinction between the terms "version" and "edition" when referring to product licenses. The term "edition" means different functional offerings within a product family that are usually released at the same time (for example, Office Professional Plus 2013 and Office Standard 2013). The term "version" refers to different generations of a product family. Downgrade rights between the current generation (*N*), the prior generation (*N-1*), and the generation prior to that (*N-2*) are limited to the same functional editions within each version (for example, Windows 8 Pro downgrades to Windows 7 Professional).

Reseller Authorization and Credibility

Sometimes enterprises enter into a triparty relationship between software manufacturer, reseller, and themselves that does not apply to all software.

The reseller may promise something or agree to something, but that normally does not change the contractual obligation of end-user obligation of the end-user organization toward the software manufacturer. The intellectual property belongs to the manufacturer, and the right to use is granted by the manufacturer, and therefore the click-wrap agreement prevails.

Beware of unethical online sellers that have taken advantage of consumers by offering drastically discounted software under the "OEM" label when it was never authorized by the publisher to be sold as such. Although there are many instances where it is perfectly legal to purchase OEM software, the phrase has often been used to trick consumers into buying counterfeit software.

More Soft Items than Software Alone

Usually software will include multiple components, and SAM needs to control all these different aspects.

1. The master copy of software itself on the master media
2. Distribution copies of the software on a freestanding media or servers
3. Software license certificates or other proof of license
4. Terms and conditions of license
5. Support contracts
6. Software pass codes or license keys

7. Software maintenance authorization codes
8. Software release documentation
9. Upgrade components
10. Installed operational instances of software

Nonexecutable Software

Copyright law protects audio, video, font, and graphics, and enterprises are vulnerable if they do not ensure compliance. In the real world, the SAM tool capabilities of this type of nonexecutable software are extremely limited. Although all the principals of SAM can be applied and used for managing the nonexecutable software life cycle, you will be required to do more manual work for compliance.

1.5 Risks to Enterprises

Legal and Financial Risks

Enterprises carry a risk if licensing terms for purchased software are not in compliance. The exposure for noncompliance may arise from enforcement agencies, industry association like BSA, SIIA and FAST, or the software manufacturer. The exposure includes the following:

1. Software being installed without license being purchased
2. Loss of proof of license for properly purchased software
3. Complex terms and conditions, which may have been violated knowingly or unknowingly
4. Contract terms with reseller were met, but license terms with manufacturer were not met

The first point is the most open exposure situation. The Business Software Alliance offers whistle-blowers rewards of up to fifty thousand dollars for reporting businesses using unlicensed software. And most of the time, it's a disgruntled ex-employee blowing the whistle. The penalties for software licensing violations can be severe. In the United States, copyright violation can be considered a civil offence or a criminal offense. The civil copyright violation—that is, unintentional violation of copyright (ignorance, mistake, error in oversight, etc.)—is up to one hundred and fifty thousand dollars on a single violation, and if you have ten different instances of the violation (say ten copies of unlicensed software), then you are exposed to a multimillion-dollar penalty.

Damaged Reputation

Brand image and reputation are very precious to all businesses these days. A potential piracy charge could seriously affect an organization's reputation. The emergence of social media and its reach and its pervasiveness may damage the reputation publicly. Within the enterprise, the IT organization's reputation would be damaged, which would put the CIO in a bad position within the organization. Loss of reputation externally results in indirect or potential erosion of business, and loss of reputation of IT internally involves erosion of cooperation and support for IT.

Unexpected Financial and Workload Impact

Right to audit is a common clause in most license agreement. It sounds logical and right, but should that audit happen, you will go through a huge and a frustrating project. These kinds of ad hoc efforts to address licensing issues in response to such external events can require an unplanned amount of time and money. About a decade ago, when Sarbanes Oxley compliance was made mandatory, organizations spend millions of dollars to establish and run audit and compliance system. The software license compliance project is comparable in time and effort.

Security Breaches

SAM is much more than license accounting and compliance. It also enables and assures that authorized and secured software is used. For example, security may be breached and confidential information may be disclosed because of inadequate patch distribution. This may lead to interruption of operation or unsupportable operation.

1.6 Benefits of SAM

Cost Saving by Better Negotiating Position

Vendors' pricing policy for the software is "what the market can bear," and every customer is not equal. If the salesperson knows your weak position on compliance, then he or she can use that position of uncertainty for compliance for obtaining the higher price. To close the deal at a higher price, a threat of audit is a very effective and often-used tool. If you know with supporting data and reports that you are compliant, you will be in better position to negotiate.

Additional Cost Saving

Besides the countering of audit threats, your position is also improved with better strategic infrastructure planning and eliminating the overdeployment of software. SAM will help you identify where software is really needed rather than where it is currently installed. SAM can also help pace the deployment with consumption and just-in-time license inventory.

More Benefits

SAM can reduce hardware cost by identifying overdeployed hardware. For example, you do not need an expensive CPU unit for a file-server system that you usually deploy for a transaction-processing system.

SAM can provide a better-priced purchase upon discovery that different organizational units at different prices and terms are purchasing the same software. You will be able to bring a better purchase strategy with SAM.

SAM will also help in controlling business risks, resulting in increased confidence of business in IT.

SAM will lead to better inventory management due to accurate information about software licenses.

Optimizing existing investments in licenses will also help IT do more with available funds. Consolidation of vendors is possible when you determine the right software needs and optimize the portfolio and avoid duplicate functionality.

1.7 SAM Challenges

Data, Data, and Data

Good data is a prerequisite for good SAM. You need trustworthy data to have good SAM, and you need good SAM to produce trustworthy data. Sounds like a vicious circle, but it is very easy to break this circle with a bootstrap approach where establishing a trustworthy database (software asset DB baseline) itself is a part of implementing SAM. Key issues with the available data are accuracy, quality, and completeness. There are two primary classes of data sources for SAM: first, the data about what you are using, and second, the data about what you have paid for. The first class of the data sources are within the IT environment, the installed software and hardware—the usage of the license. The second class of the data sources are outside the IT environment—the contracts and agreements, purchase orders, invoices, and so on. Most SAM solutions focus on the first source via discovery tools and technologies; however, the second part is a matter of non-IT business processes. Depending upon the business practices of the organization, it could be very easy to obtain or be very difficult because of widely distributed record keeping without a link between them.

It is very important to understand that there will be multiple data sources to feed your SAM system, and you must establish a data-collection strategy—which data will come from where and how the accuracy and completeness of the data at source will be assured, as well as who will own the data and maintain the data at source.

Typical problems in data management are these:

1. **Inadequate purchase data:** The purchase orders are prepared to track the dollars and not the software. The kind of information required in a PO may be insufficient for tracking licenses. The purchase record should be the authentic source of the information, such as the following:

    a. Number of licenses procured

    b. Type of licenses procured

    c. Product information as per purchase record

    d. Licensing model for the product

    e. Product suite information—components of the product

    f. License upgrade information—freely upgradable or not

    g. Asset allocation information

    h. Asset ownership information

2. **Raw data:** The volume of raw data from discovery is overwhelming primarily because of the IT tendency to use the tool for what it can discover, rather then what you are targeting to discover.
3. **Dynamic environment:** The environment changes continuously, and processes to maintain the currency of the data may not be sufficient.
4. **Lack of executive sponsorship:** This affects not just the SAM but the holistic program that has touch points on almost all operational parts of IT.

1.8 SAM Solution: Desired Functionality

A full-scale SAM solution should deliver the following functionalities:

Compliance management: This is the most important requirement of SAM. The solution should be able to produce the compliance report. These reports should be trustworthy; therefore, the solution should have the capability to create and maintain a trustworthy dataset. This is indeed a big deal. So easy to say and so difficult to do! The derivative features for this functionality will include these:

1. Electronic storage of software license certificates or other proof of licenses
2. Maintenance of software inventory
3. Maintenance of product catalogs/signatures
4. Maintenance of PO, support contracts, and terms and conditions of licenses

License-cost optimization: Cost optimization can be done simply by license harvesting and eliminating the financial waste of unused licenses. The solution should have the capability to reclaim the licenses from the retired machines and the ability to detect unused licenses. More mature solutions will have the capability to optimize the cost by analyzing the environment and determining alternate licensing models without losing the business capability of the software. License-model and license-term analysis capability like upgrading and downgrading the path of software and its components is required.

DSL, the single source of truth: A premium solution will also include the functionality of DSL (definite software library). DSL is a big deal. Creating a DSL is a big project, and maintaining a DSL is hard and intelligent work as well. DSL functionality will automatically enforce maturity in the whole-process ecosystem, including sourcing the software (demand-management and procurement process), building and packaging the software (SDLC and release management), and deploying the software (change and deployment management). Additionally, a DSL will also automatically bring in the following features:

1. Maintenance of a master copy of software itself on the master media
2. Maintenance of information for all authorized deployed software
3. Maintenance of software license keys

The functionality of DSL has a cascading effect on additional functionality. For example, you will be required to create and maintain an approved list of software to drive integrity in the demand-and-procurement processes.

Security and controls: Security controls are a matter of developing policies, maintaining policies, institutionalizing policies, and enforcing policies in a plausible manner. Security and controls is a desirable functionality that will bring in features like prevention of unauthorized software use as well as unauthorized use of approved software.

1.9 SAM in the Context of the Cloud

SAM for a cloud service provider is different than the SAM within the enterprise. This book is entirely focused on the SAM within enterprise IT. Of course, we expect that a portion of the enterprise landscape would include the public cloud as well as the private cloud. For the public cloud, the liability of license management of the software that comes with the public-cloud service is with the cloud service provider; therefore, enterprises do not need to worry about software in the cloud, as they are merely using software as a service. It is different for the private cloud; the accountability of any other software being installed on that public-cloud instance still is with the enterprise. For example, if you buy an Amazon EC2 instance running Windows Server 2012, the OS license is provided by Amazon, but any other add-on services like active directory or database-like SQL server responsibility is with the enterprise. In case of a SaaS service, the entire stack is provided by the SaaS provider; hence only external systems are what enterprise needs to license as owned and managed by enterprise IT, and we will discuss the adjustments required in the traditional SAM to accommodate private-cloud SAM.

License in Virtualization Environment versus Cloud Environment

Virtualization helps reduce complexity by reducing the number of physical hosts, but it still involves purchasing servers and software and maintaining your infrastructure. Its greatest benefit is reducing the cost of that infrastructure for companies by maximizing the usage of physical resources.

While virtualization may be used to provide cloud computing, cloud computing is quite different from virtualization. Cloud computing may look like virtualization because it appears that your application is running on a virtual server detached from any reliance or connection to a single physical host. And they are similar in that fashion. However, cloud computing can be better described as a service where virtualization is part of a physical infrastructure. Besides this, "cloud" means an extremely dynamic environment where servers have a short life cycle. So if you are using 100 licenses today, you may be using 120 tomorrow. This makes the license accounting entirely different if you choose a standard instance-based licensing model.

1.10 SAM in the Context of BYOD

BYOD (bring your own device) is gaining popularity and momentum. BYOD is an IT policy that allows an employee to use his/her personal laptop and mobile devices to access enterprise data and systems. There could be two kind of controls in BYOD—control over the central resources that are controlled by IT (*what* is allowed to access) and, second, control over the accessing device (*how* it is allowed to access, either using a licensed client or a generic browser or client that does not need a license).

The first control is primarily the security domain that will decide the policy and manage the security aspects—unlimited access or access only to nonsensitive systems and data. Security concerns will also need to account for unauthorized use of network access—for example, the corporate network can be used to access the public Internet and carry out unauthorized activities. The second kind of control is the area of interest to SAM also, especially because of the following:

1. It may incur the liability of license for the application that is being accessed by the device.
2. IT is providing the license of the client software to access the application.

The license metering in the first scenario is maintained at the central level, so it does not pose much of a problem.

Most often, software installed on user-owned devices do not cause any liability of financial or legal compliances on the enterprises. However, there could be some deviations. In order to protect their own network from viruses, many enterprises buy end-point protection software and provide it to personal devices under a valid license term. From a SAM perspective it is a matter of financial accounting rather than a compliance liability. Regardless, IT will be required to have control over the user-owned device.

What if a license is bought by enterprise and given to a BYOD owner who then quits? Enterprise software should have rights to be extended to nonemployee users like temp workers/contractors, and the responsibility of provisioning and deprovisioning is with the enterprise. There are methods like application virtualization/application streaming/virtual desktop, which are examples of methods to enforce BYOD licensing.

Stolen software from enterprises: If the software has been stolen intentionally, the individual will be held legally responsible; however, the license-compliance contract between the licensee and licensor will determine the liability for the enterprise, which is one gray zone in SAM.

Home-use scheme: If the BYOD user has purchased software to use on his or her device, the user can use it in any scenario permitted by the license. However, if the software needs some enterprise add-on/access license, then the enterprise has to provision for the same. For example, a Windows machine with Microsoft Office Home Premium would have Outlook for use with public e-mail services; however, to use Enterprise Exchange and Windows Core Services, the enterprise would need to license for Core CAL and E-CAL additionally. However, new offerings like Microsoft Office 365 are trying to bridge some of these gaps by providing dual-use licensing options.

2 HOLISTIC SAM SOLUTION ARCHITECTURE

Figure 2 shows the holistic SAM architecture. This represents the most matured state, and an organization may choose to implement a part of it according to their need.

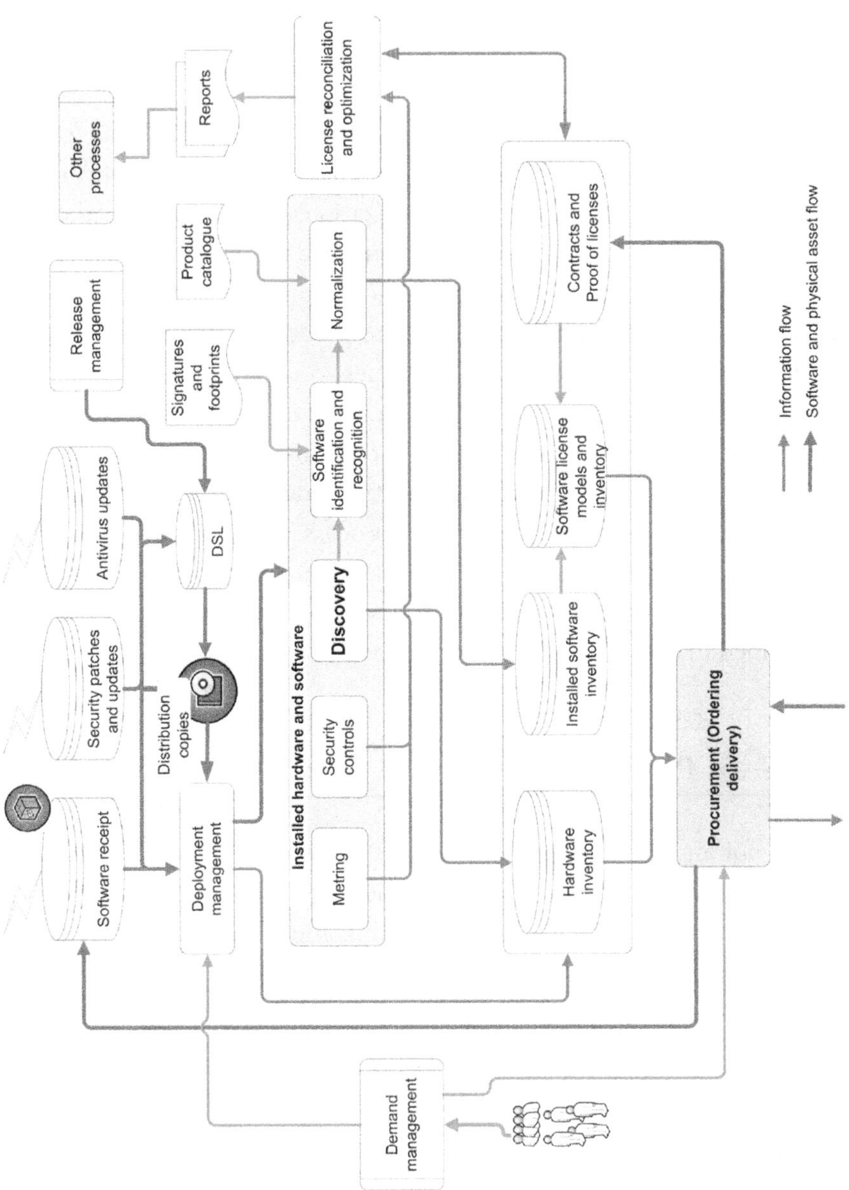

Figure 2. SAM architecture

The appendix provides a sample tool-set list that maps with this architecture.

2.1 Overview of the Architecture

SAM uses discovery to create the inventory of hardware and software. Software-identification techniques are used to recognize and identify installed software in scope for SAM. After normalization, SAM determines the correct installed base. The software in use as determined by metering and normalized data is compared with the entitlement provided by the contracts and license models, and finally varieties of reports are produced. These reports not only provide compliance evidence but also clues to usage optimization and cost saving. Reports may trigger several action items through other processes—for example, uninstall software, purchase extra license, change the license model. DSL maintains the authorized copy of software deployed through deployment management of the release-management process. All software receipts are verified and stored in DSL in installable pack form. Demand management deals with the new demands of software and triggers the deployment process. This is explained in detail in subsequent sections.

2.2 SAM Process Ecosystem

SAM is not an individual process but a comprehensive set of integrated processes. Industry guidance such as ITIL and ISO (international standard organization) has variation in the process organization, but as a complete set they map to the same outcome.

2.2.1 ITIL and SAM

The areas associated with SAM are included in a distributed manner in ITIL V2 books (*Service Delivery, Service Support, Application Management, and Security Management*, although the ICT Infrastructure Management and Business Perspective book is also involved to lesser extent). In 2003, OGC (office of government commerce) created a separate book dedicated to SAM that combined distributed tips into one single coherent approach for SAM. ITIL V3 also provides distributed tips in various service-life-cycle stages, but a dedicated publication (after three years of ITIL V2 book publication) still remains the focused ITIL book on SAM. Figure 3 presents the ITIL process set that enables SAM.

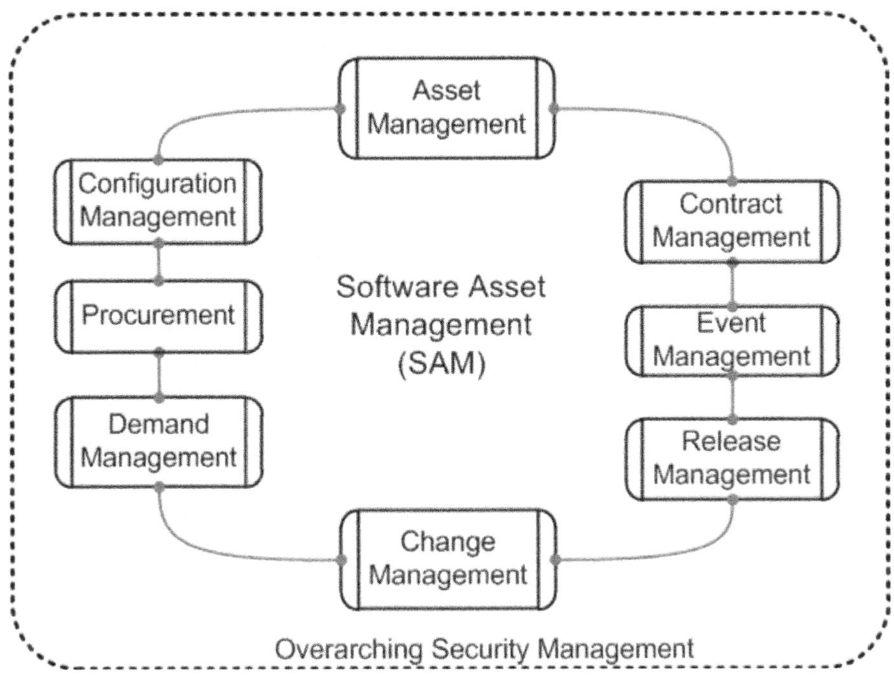

Figure 3. ITIL process ecosystem for SAM

ITIL SAM Framework

ITIL divides SAM into five process areas, and each area has multiple processes, as shown in Figure 4.

Overall management processes

- Overall management Responsibility
- Risk Assessment
- Policies and procedures
- Competence, awareness and training
- Performance metrics and continuous improvements
- Service continuity and availability management

Core asset-management processes

- Asset identification
- Asset control
- Status accounting
- Database management
- Financial management

Logistics processes

- Requirement definition
- Design
- Evaluation
- Procurement
- Build
- Deployment
- Operation
- Optimization
- Retirement

Verification and compliance processes

- Verification and audit
- Licensing compliance
- Security compliance
- Other compliance

Relationship processes

- Contract management
- Supplier management
- Internal business-relationship management
- Outsourcing management

Figure 4. ITIL SAM area

The Process Ecosystem

We think of SAM as a kind of process ecosystem that works together, and imbalance in any one process would affect the SAM results. The following provides a brief explanation of each process in this ecosystem and how it affects SAM outcome.

Asset management: Asset management is, of course, the nucleus of SAM. Asset management includes an asset database—hardware as well as software—and the surrounding control processes to maintain accuracy and currency. As stated earlier, it is impossible to manage software assets without also managing the hardware on which the software runs; therefore, hardware-asset management becomes an integral part of SAM. An asset database is different than CMDB, although they do have common data.

Configuration management: Configuration management includes CMDB and surrounding processes to maintain the accuracy and currency of CMDB. The big difference between the asset DB and CMDB is that CMDB maintains the relationship between the CIs. In the SAM context, the installed product is a CI and related to the hardware. An asset database, on the other hand, maintains the financial and contract data, which is also needed for SAM.

Demand management: Demand management deals with user demand as well as the business demand for the software licenses. Demand management interfaces with SAM to provide the necessary information to update the license database. Demand may or may not trigger the purchase process.

Change management: Change management is the primary control for CMDB. Installation of new hardware or software or amendment in an existing environment may alter the license accounting. If you upgrade the hardware, for example, the license model may change. Change management helps SAM to maintain and account for changing usage of software.

Release management: Release management creates the new deployment package or alters the existing deployment packages. The content of the deployment pack are important to understand, and appropriate license-accounting methods must be applied.

Event management: Event management refers to the monitoring and control process for service monitoring. You detect an event and create an alarm for error conditions. This process is usually used to monitor the installation of unauthorized software.

2.2.2 ISO Framework for SAM

ISO divides the framework into three core process areas:

1. Organizational management processes for SAM
2. Core SAM processes
3. Primary process interfaces for SAM

Each of these areas has multiple processes and subprocesses, as given in Figure 5.

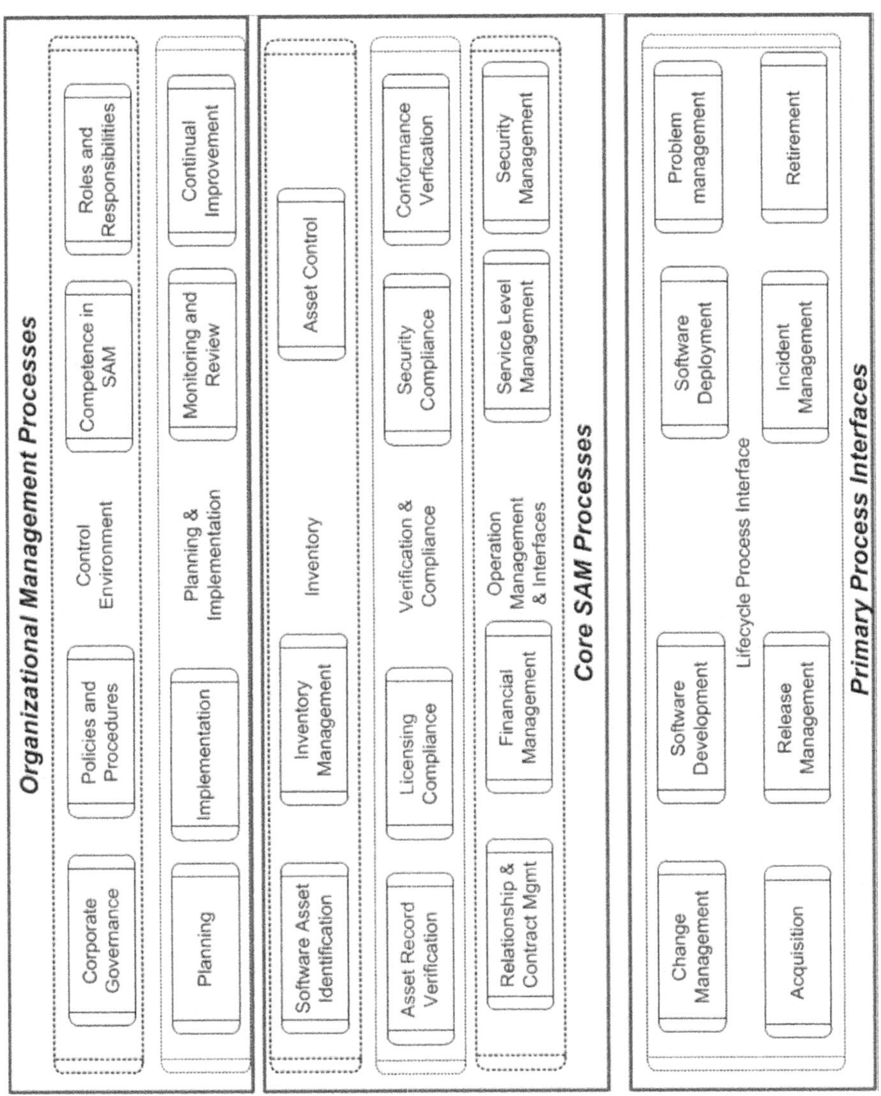

Figure 5. ISO SAM process ecosystem

ISO has a different process definition—for example, we consider deployment as a part of release, but ISO specifies release and deployment separately. From the functional perspective, both ITIL and ISO form a complete ecosystem.

3 HOLISTIC SOLUTION SUBSYSTEMS

3.1 Discovery

Trustworthy data is the foundation of SAM, and the first step as well as the very core need is to create and maintain an inventory database. The inventory baseline is built with multiple data sources, and the discovery is the primary data source.

Discovery provides the information related to **what exists** in the environment. Industry has wide variety of tools for discovery. Usually the way to discover installed software is file scans, ARP/registry, WMI, and other probes and ISO tags. ISO tags are wonderful in delivering accurate data, and we discuss this in detail later in this section. ISO tag adoption is currently limited and progressing with a slow pace. Discovery is most often used for CMDB, but there is a difference between discovery for CMDB and discovery for SAM. In fact, the discovery depth needed for SAM is much less than that for CMDB. SAM needs to know the one-tier relationship—that is, the relationship between the hardware and the installed software. It does not care about the relationship between two software CIs—for example, the relationship of application with database. For CMDB the relationship between any to any CI is essential need. Similarly, the discovery for monitoring the managed objects in a CI is different than the discovery for SAM. The discovery needs and instrumentation for monitoring depend on the object you want to monitor.

There are two method of reaching out to the target system and fetching the data—agent based and agentless. The following table explains the comparison.

Agent Based	Agentless
An agent is physically installed on the device.	Agent is executed remotely on the device.
Admin access is required for agents to install.	No admin access is required for agentless approach.
It provides more in-depth information of software installed.	Information fetched depends on the probes.
Change-management process is required as agent is getting deployed.	There are less change-management/ build process concerns as no code is being deployed.
Consumes system resources.	There is no system resource consumption.
Recommended for end-user assets.	Recommended for data-center assets.

Discovery can also be run in two modes—scheduled mode and on-demand mode. The scheduled mode runs the discovery job and collects the data at the specified schedule, which can be configured according to need. Typically for SAM, even a quarterly discovery would be good enough. However, in some cases, organizations might be paying the software vendors on a monthly subscription basis; therefore, at least a monthly discovery would become necessary. If the SAM is very well matured, then on-demand discovery would be common.

Application Instrumentation and Discovery

Instrumentation defines how an application will expose itself for the discovery. Windows Management Instrumentation (WMI) is the Microsoft application of the Web-Based Enterprise Management initiative for an industry standard for accessing management information. Most application vendors design adequate instrumentation for discovering their applications; however, you may end up with certain applications not getting discovered. Homegrown applications are the most likely candidates for such scenarios. If homegrown applications are not getting discovered, it will not affect the legal-compliance aspect of SAM (you do not buy a license as you are owner of the application), but it will affect CMDB significantly more as you will not be able to see the application and relation in CMDB.

Discovery Considerations

Implementing discovery is often underestimated from the perspective of time and effort. When technical experts give the time and effort estimates, they usually focus on the tool part only and ignore the environmental and operational prerequisites, as well as the contributions required from the other groups, especially the application teams. Agent-based discovery is desirable to obtain the greater level of information for installed software. Installation of agents is a big exercise in any organization. Access to the target devices and opening of firewall ports both require security approval. In addition, the actual deployment in a distributed environment is time-consuming.

If you do not configure the discovery efficiently, you will have overwhelming data to deal with. More data is good for SAM, but not the raw data. Do not get carried away with the tool capability and be tempted to pick up data you will not use. On the other side, you will also face the issue of incomplete data because the reach of discovery may not be 100%.

Discovery Output

After a successful discovery and identification, you have fairly good information about these topics:

- What devices are in use
- Which software is being used
- Who is using the software
- How often the software is used

Discovery Limitations

Discovery tools cannot discover everything that you need. There are technical limitations like target device or target CI instrumentation. Some devices like network security control devices and some storage devices are nondiscoverable by most of the discovery tools.

You will be required to add some data elements like location and business owner manually. Location data becomes important if you have site licenses specific to geography.

Mobile device discovery has more limitations because the technology is relatively new. However, mobile device management (MDM) tools are gaining maturity with a fast pace, and discovery is an integral part of these tools.

Discovery Challenges

The biggest challenge in discovery is nontechnical. Data-center devices are governed by strict access control. Detailed discovery may require privileged access, which will require security approvals in any organization. Further, you will also need a specific port for communication between the discovery server and the device even if it is agentless discovery. Agent-based discovery will require installation of the agent on each target device. These are all manageable challenges, yet take time and effort.

3.2 *Software Identification and Recognition*

Discovery and identification are two different kinds of data processing for different purposes, but both are performed together in the SAM process. The discovery tool provides the data, and identification converts that data into information and knowledge. Discovery is primarily for data collection, and identification is to single out what data it is.

3.2.1 Identification Basics

Product versus Installation

A software product has a name and version and is delivered in a set of files that are not executable. Signatures and the footprints of the software product are associated with an installation and identify each product name and version when the product is installed. Footprints like ***.exe*** and ***.dll*** files are created during installation.

The discovery tool usually picks up the data from two sources, and there are problems with each:

File Header Information

File headers contain meta-information such as name, version, author, and so forth regarding the content of the file. File headers are placed inside a block in the beginning of the file (not necessarily starting on the very first line), one header per line. A header consists of a name and a value. Titles and descriptions are the name and value of the header. Unfortunately, titles and descriptions used to describe the software application at the time of packaging or compiling do not follow industry convention and vary from vendor to vendor.

Add/Remove Program Data/Registry Entry

1. Inaccurate and incomplete information can be discovered as the installation utilities are not standard.
2. Installation utilities have their own method of making the program ready for execution. The process varies for each program and each computer; therefore, programs and operating systems, as well, often need a specialized program for doing whatever is needed for their installation. Installation may be part of a larger software-deployment process.
3. During the installation, code are copied or generated from the installation files to new files on the local computer. Different parts of the codes are copied or generated in different locations in the local computer. A typical installation job includes at least the following:
   a. Creating or updating program files and folders
   b. Adding configuration data such as configuration files, Windows registry entries, or environment variables
   c. Making the software accessible to the user—for instance, by creating links, shortcuts, or bookmarks
   d. Configuring components that run automatically, such as daemons or Windows services
4. Uninstallation usually involves more than just erasing the program folder. For example, registry files need to be deleted for a complete uninstallation.

Discovery and identification using software ID tags eliminates almost all these problems and performs wonderful identification. This is the most powerful signature for all software products. It is an exciting initiative by ISO, and the next section is dedicated to it.

3.2.2 Software ID Tags

ISO/IEC 19770-2 provides international standards for software identification tags, but these were published in 2009, and adoption is very slow. These tags provide a universal and standard way to identify software and simplify the process of tracking and managing the software. This ISO standard greatly simplifies the software-identification process, helping lower the cost of managing software licenses for most customers. This is an important first step in making it easier for customers to manage their software assets.

Although software license compliance is the most important part of software asset management, SAM scope is much more than just matching software use to entitlements. SAM is also a key strategy to help organizations ensure they receive maximum value from their software while minimizing risks.

What do software ID tags do?

1. Software identification tags provide the meta-data necessary to support more accurate identification—significantly better than traditional file-oriented identification techniques.
2. Software ID tags identify suites of software products just like individual software products. This helps manage suites as effectively as individual products.

3. Software ID tags are now the de facto standard between different software creators, and within software-creator organizations, of how different versions of software are identified.
4. Software ID tags make an automated approach to license compliance, using information both from the software identification tag and from the software entitlement tag, feasible.
5. Software ID tags provide comprehensive information about the structural footprint of packages—i.e., the list of components such as files and system settings associated with that package.
6. Software ID tags provide information about usage of software and help to deal with the complexities of software installed on removable or shared storage or in virtual environments.
7. Software ID tags can verify authenticity through the use of digital signatures by anyone creating or modifying information in the software identification tag.
8. Independent providers, or in-house personnel if originally not created by the software creator, can create software ID tags.

Tag Details

These software identification tags are simply small XML data files that are installed with the software. They contain seven mandatory data elements and thirty-one optional data elements:

1. Product title
2. Product version
3. Software creator
4. Software licensor

5. Tag creator
6. Unique software identifier
7. Entitlement required (yes/no)

Optional Data Elements in Software Tags	
1. abstract 2. component_of 3. complex_of 4. data_source 5. dependency 6. elements_owner 7. installation_details 8. keywords 9. license_linkage 10. package_footprint 11. packager 12. product_category 13. product_family 14. product_id 15. release_date 16. release_id	17. release_package 18. release_rollout 19. release_verification 20. serial_number 21. sku 22. software_creator_alias 23. software_licensor_alias 24. supported_languages 25. tag_creator_alias 26. tag_creator_copyright 27. tag_version 28. upgrade_for 29. usage_identifier 30. validation 31. ds: Signature
For details go to http://standards.iso.org/iso/19770/-2/2009/schema.xsd. Published by International Standard Organization (www.iso.org)	

These software ID tags are XML data files that are installed with software. They are simply markers, which indicate what software has been installed. These tags do not report back to software vendors, nor do they verify license rights. They are intended to be a tool that can provide customers with better insight into the software that they are using in order to lower the costs of managing those software assets.

Software ID tags provide information that helps find accurate data concerning software inventory. They do not include information about the specific license entitlements or metrics involved with that software; however, having accurate inventory information is the first step in successfully determining your license requirements.

Who should use tags?

Platform providers: Those who provide platforms for running software (hardware, OS, or a virtual environment) should provide tag-management capabilities at their level.

Software providers: Software creators, software packagers, or software licensors that provide software for distribution or installation should comply with software ID tags to help software asset management and make it consumer friendly. They can use "tag providers" who create or modify software identification tags.

Tag providers: A tag provider is a tag creator and may be part of the software-provider organization or may be a third-party organization or the software consumer.

Tag tool providers: These are the entities that may provide any number of tools that create, modify, or use software identification tags.

Software consumers: These are the entities that consume software and are the major beneficiaries of the software identification tag.

How does it work?

Figure 6 explains how the tags work.

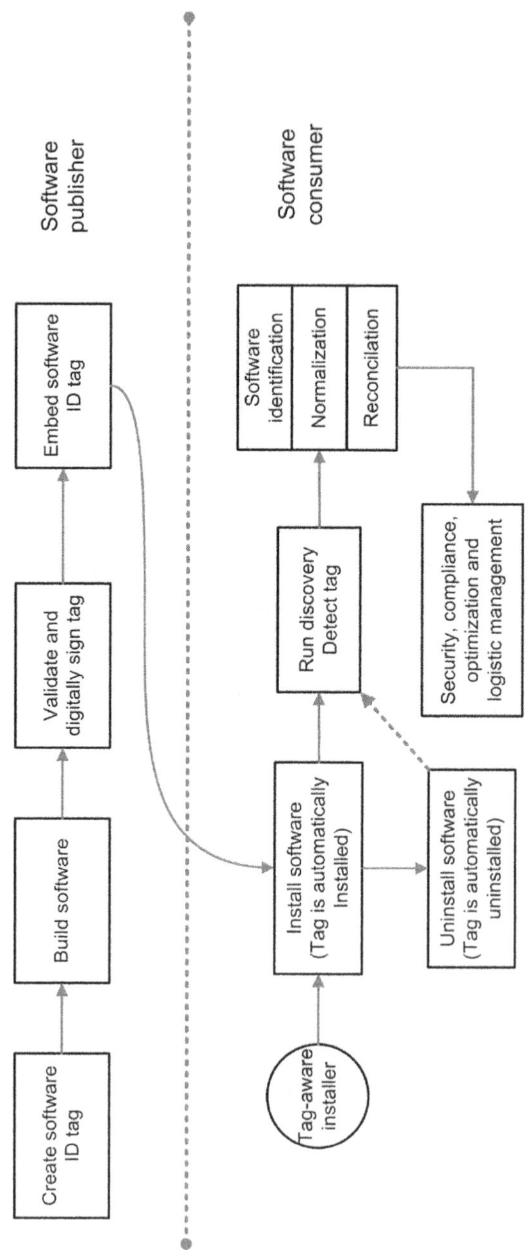

Figure 6. How SWID tags work

Current Industry Scenarios

Many discovery and SAM tool providers have started bringing in features in their tools to take advantage of software ID tags. Altiris, Aspera License Management, CA Technologies discovery tools, Eracent's EnterpriseAM, Flexera Software's FlexNet Manager Platform, HP's DDMI and Software Management Suite, and Microsoft's System Center 2012 R2 Configuration Manager are among the popular tools that are currently supporting it.

On the other hand, major software vendors have started adding tags in their products. Major vendors like Microsoft, IBM, CA, and HP are starting to embed tags in their products.

3.3 *Normalization*

Normalization **identifies** what exists in the environment. It matches software install data with software product catalog rationalized and presented in an accurate, unified, and truly meaningful manner.

What does normalization do?

1. **Weeds out duplicates:** The same software application identified by different names will appear as different entries in the discovery tool raw data. Normalization brings all those entries under one standard name. Normalization uses product catalog as a common dictionary.
2. **Provides suite recognition:** An application suite generally consists of two or more software programs of related functionality, delivered within a single executable and installable file. An application suite contains software from a single software publisher and encapsulates it into a layer of executable program. The installer enables the

installation of the suite applications individually, or the entire software stack can be installed at once. It may not be obvious that the software is a part of a suite and may appear as an independent product. Normalization identifies if the software is an independent standalone product or a module of a suite.

3. **Offers bundle recognition:** Software bundles are similar to the suite except that the individual products in the bundle may or may not be related. Further, they may not be from the same publisher, and an installer may not be able to install them as a bundle and individual installation may be required. For all practical purposes, they are independent except for the license model. Some applications have bundles or include other OEM software, which might look like a full installation, and normalization uses the product catalog library information to recognize.
4. **Accounts for incomplete uninstall:** Sometimes you may uninstall software and reclaim the software license. If, during uninstallation, you do not purge the file or do not follow the prescribed procedures for uninstall, then the traces will declare that the software exists. Normalization, using signature and footprints, detects and accounts for uninstalled software.
5. **Normalization** also takes care of duplicate installation, partial installation, and version variations.

Product Catalog and Recognition Algorithm

One of the most common problems is the difference in the names and descriptions of the same software found by discovery and listed in purchase orders. A product catalog makes everyone speak the same language. It aligns the naming convention and description of the product across all life-cycle management. The richness of a product catalog is one of the important selling points of a SAM tool. A product catalog also enriches the discovered data with version and maintenance property—for example, patch or upgrade requirements of the discovered software. A product catalog needs constant maintenance and updates as new products come in and old products retire.

In the SAM world, it is an important dataset, and now vendors are available who provide this data as a service. BDNA, a prominent SAM player, offers its product catalog as a service. In its product catalog, BDNA categorizes and aligns over one million hardware and software products and updates to two thousand data points daily to ensure it is current and complete. Definitely, your environment will not require exhaustive catalog. In fact, for limited scope, you can develop your own product catalog from the raw data of discovery tools.

Even if you buy the most comprehensive, current, and accurate product catalog, you may consider enriching it further with custom application in your environment. However, it may not be necessary for compliance purposes as you will not be interested in license management of your bespoke applications.

A product catalog with software signatures, footprints, as well as algorithms, groups and correlates all executable (.exe) files and dynamic-link libraries (.dlls) to a single application. In this way the scanned raw data is converted into meaningful information that includes the name and description.

Challenges

Because of a lack of standardization, the recognition rules have limitations and cannot be applied to all software. Manual intervention is required to interpret some of the data. As discussed in section 4.2.2, software ID tags, the ISO standard, will address this problem. The software identification, recognition, and enrichment of a catalog will be greatly simplified and will enable significant automation.

SAM Result Dependency

The contributors for the best result normalizations are these:

1. Capabilities of the discovery tools
2. Reach of discovery tools
3. How the discovery is configured and implemented
4. The product catalog quality
5. The software recognition method

3.4 Metering

Metering is applying the instrumentation for the measurement of the license metric. There are two aspects of it. One is the existence of the license product, and second is the consumption pattern. Metering focuses on the measurement of consumption as per the license metric. You will need the right instrumentation built in the SAM tool for such measurement. Most discovery tools also provide the data points for metering.

- Metering reflects the consumption pattern.
- Metering provides software inventory details of all software installed in the organization with details such as frequently used, occasionally used, or rarely used.

Software metering provides comprehensive and detailed software-usage statistics that help you avoid purchasing additional licenses or renewing contracts for the applications that are not being utilized. By identifying unused software, you can reallocate copies to users who truly need them or renegotiate software contracts so they reflect actual usage—saving your organization significant amounts of money.

Metering is an intelligence gathering for license optimization. Modern metering technologies capabilities help you do the following:

1. Determine how often specific applications are being used
2. Determine who is using those applications
3. Identify unused and underutilized licenses
4. Discover if there are unauthorized, harmful, or "nuisance" applications
5. Collect detailed software-usage statistics including start time, stop time, idle time, and peak usage

3.5 *Reconciliation*

Reconciliation is the process of matching the entitlement with the usage. Simply, it is a comparison of what and how much you bought versus what and how much you are using. Reconciliation is not easy because software licensing can be very complex and potentially confusing for the customer. Software licensing models are constantly evolving to keep pace with hardware innovation.

Use of technologies such as virtualization can affect licensing requirements, and each software vendor has a different model for virtual environments. Reconciling license on virtualized environments is often difficult due to their scalable nature and daily or even hourly changes. Reconciliation logic is different in a guest system running individually or on a cluster and whether the physical resources are limited or unlimited.

Most software companies offer a wide range of license models. All vendors believe in providing more variety and more choices to the customers. Unfortunately, those choices are not for the products but for the commercial models, and we believe that more choices in licensing models are creating more problems than solving.

Some software may need additional components to be licensed separately. This is a very simple sentence to write in the contract but very complex to deal with during reconciliation.

Gone are the days of very simple license models such as device-based and user-based models, where you could do the reconciliation with the help of Microsoft Excel worksheets.

A reconciliation engine, which is a part of advanced SAM tools, computes the usage of licenses and compares with the entitlement as per the software vendor's licensing contract using a reconciliation algorithm. It maintains the algorithm for each type of licensing model and corresponding computation logic. Reconciliation-engine capabilities differ from SAM solution vendors. Most ITSM (IT service management) tools offer capability of computation on four basic models—user based, device based, CPU core based, and access based. Advanced SAM tools have capabilities for almost all kinds of reconciliation algorithm.

Reconciliation gives the effective consumption or usage and the compliance information. License reconciliation is required to achieve the **compliance** as well as the **usage** information of the procured license rights versus the entitled and installed licenses.

Reconciliation—Consideration

Reconciliation invariably will be done in multiple iterations. Consider the following points while preparing for the reconciliation:

1. **The number of licensing models the tool can handle:** This is one of the tool-selection criteria also.

2. **The number of clear and unambiguous licensing models in your contracts:** It is a tedious work to go through the agreement and derive a correct, clear, and unambiguous license model and metric.
3. **The number of ambiguous licensing models in your contracts:** The language of the agreement may not help to arrive at the right model, and you may need to collaborate with the vendor to interpret it correctly.
4. **The number of datasets and the possibility of segregation:** SAM data repositories are usually distributed.
5. **Number of the products in scope:** Volume of the data.

Reconciliation—Benefits

Reconciliation is the foundation for license-management processes, and compliance is the primary goal, but reconciliation can deliver additional benefits such as these:

1. Basis for license agreement negotiations
2. Redistribution of unused software licenses
3. Detailed overview serves as basis for migration planning

3.6 Security and Controls

The goal of security defines the goal of the SAM, and controls are the methods used to achieve the goals. Typical controls will be policies, processes, and functions (organizational structure). A few examples of control processes are the following:

1. Prevention of installation of unauthorized software
2. Detection and removal of unauthorized software
3. Harvesting of unused licenses
4. Reclamation of software against disposed hardware
5. Building the IT-approved software catalog and forcing selection only from the approved catalog

Each process will also include a set of policies. In section 5.6 we discuss more policies and processes.

3.6.1 Security and Controls—Challenges

The very first challenge involves the technology constraints and/or financial constraints. Either the technology is not available to implement the policies beyond paper, or it is prohibitively expensive. Although tools are gaining capabilities and maturity rapidly, the complexity of the environment is growing even more rapidly. So tools are always in the catching-up game.

SAM strategy is an important aspect where you will have tools and process strategies. You should choose optimal capabilities of tools and keep in mind that tools will not solve process problems.

The second challenge is completely nontechnical. Noncompliance is deemed as piracy, and security and controls to prevent piracy imply the monitoring as well as policing of your devices for what software is being used and for what purpose. In fact, because of financial aspects of software assets, security controls also police when it was used and how it was used. We all believe in freedom and feel uneasy if someone is spying on or policing us. There might be some tendency of noncooperation on SAM policies and processes. This is one of the biggest challenges.

You can consider an approach of community policing. Community policing is a philosophy that promotes organizational SAM strategies, which support the systematic use of partnerships and problem-solving techniques, to proactively address the risks of unauthorized use of software and use of unauthorized software. It is a collaborative partnership between the SAM group and the end users of the software. The basic theme is recognizing that the SAM group alone cannot solve problems and encouraging interactive partnerships with users. Creation of focus groups among user-community members who are volunteering (because of some incentive) as partners can be used to accomplish the goals by gaining a perspective of the problem from the other side, engaging in collaborative problem solving, and improving trust and cooperation.

3.7 *Optimization*

The goal of optimization is to bring in value for money by ensuring that the licenses are utilized in the most cost-effective manner. Optimization also helps compliance by bringing usage within the entitlement limit. This is very analogous to the capacity management of SAM. Optimization is closely related to compliance; if licenses do not have sufficient entitlements, the organization would be out of compliance.

Basic optimization methods are simple and straightforward coming out from the reconciliation reports. These include uninstallation of unused software and uninstallation of overused software—in other words, the number that exceeds the entitlement. Further, basic optimization will also do a trend analysis to determine future license needs and deployment pace and save money. Basic optimization will also include harvesting and reclamation as general controls that are discussed in other sections.

Advanced optimization includes the simulation of operating environments and explores license alternatives. Advanced SAM tools support techniques like what-if scenarios and help leverage existing contracts and licenses to reduce costs. With the help of advanced optimization techniques, you can systematically reduce software spending.

Major software manufacturers have developed increasingly complex ways to record and charge for software usage in their licensing contracts. Such metrics include models like Named user plus (Oracle), Concurrent usage (Citrix), and processor- or core-dependent licensing (IBM, Oracle, Microsoft). Simple trend analysis and basic formulae have limitations for optimization. Simulation and what-if scenario analysis is a great feature available to optimize the complex license model.

Optimization Benefits

- Optimize efficiencies with centralized asset tracking to know what software is owned, what could be better used elsewhere, and what types of software will be required in the future
- Optimize negotiations and vendor relations by knowing exactly what software the organization needs and uses
- Optimize the time to market through streamlined software functionality and a thorough knowledge of existing databases
- Optimize the cost of licenses by determining the most optimal licensing model—e.g., floating versus fixed license or user versus site licenses

3.8 Definitive Software Library

DSL is the ITIL concept. Definitive software library ITIL is the library in which the definitive authorized versions of all software CIs are stored and protected. It is a physical library or storage repository where master copies of software versions are placed. This one logical storage area may, in reality, consist of one or more physical software libraries or file stores. They should be separate from development and test file-store areas. The definitive software library ITIL may also include a physical store to hold master copies of procurred software. Only authorized software should be accepted into the DSL, strictly controlled by change and release management.

DSL supports one important SAM goals that only correctly released and authorized versions are in use. The definitive software library ITIL should do the following:

1. Only contain authorized versions of software
2. Be totally separate from all other software development, testing, or live area
3. Hold secure copies of package software
4. Keep all software up to date and free from corruption
5. Be accessible only to software control and distribution staff
6. Document the status of all stored software versions

Managing DSL

How software will enter into DSL, and how its record will be maintained, is a critical SAM control. DSL management includes these:

- **Acquiring new software:** Software acquisition will be the responsibility of procurement process under the policies of SAM. Once the software is received or downloaded, it will go through verification and testing and then make its way to DSL.
- **Retiring software packages:** Since DSL is the current operational inventory of the authorized software, the retired software should be disabled from access as well as for modification or update of corresponding record.

- **Copying software from the library:** SAM policy may allow copying of software for some specific purpose as allowed by the vendors. In any case you will ensure that the integrity of the original is maintained.

Value of DSL

DSL enables the integrity of the software deployed in the production and brings in the consistency of all the installed instances. By controlling the consistency of the source at DSL, you can control the software in the environment—for example, removing software from the library will prevent deployments of retired software.

Prevention of wrong software deployment eliminates the business risk. As a general policy, organizations would not deploy out-of-support software. There may be exceptions. DSL is the primary instrument to provide this assurance.

DSL makes compliance easy because you have the authorized and single source of truth.

3.9 Databases

We have repeatedly emphasized trustworthy data. The SAM system will have multiple databases that will collectively form the trustworthy dataset. CMDB alone cannot serve the purpose of SAM, but it can very well be one of the data sources. Completeness and accuracy are the prime attributes of trustworthy data. One single data source does not provide the required quality—completeness and correctness. You may have multiple discovery tools for different purposes—for example, most organizations have different tools for end-user environment discovery and data-center environment discovery. You might have built a good CMDB, but we have observed that the CMDB does not contain the required data for the purpose of SAM. From a SAM perspective, the utilities, development tools, and other software in the development environment are also important, but from a CMDB perspective they are not important.

Discovery and CMDB also provide the SAP environment data, but that may not be adequate for SAM. Therefore, you would need to use LMDB in SAP environment as the data source for the trustworthy data feed to SAM. SAP LMDB is discussed later in section 7.2.

Similarly, discovery and CMDB do have data from the virtual environment, but vCenter database is the most trustworthy data source for SAM. We approach this in section 7.1.

While we are assuming that these data sources are individually trustworthy data sources, collectively they may be inconsistent. This is usually because of these being asynchronous systems. For example, you assigned a user some license or device, and later the user was deleted from the active directory, but that information was not reconciled.

Typical Data Flow

Figure 7 explains how the data flows from various sources to the SAM database.

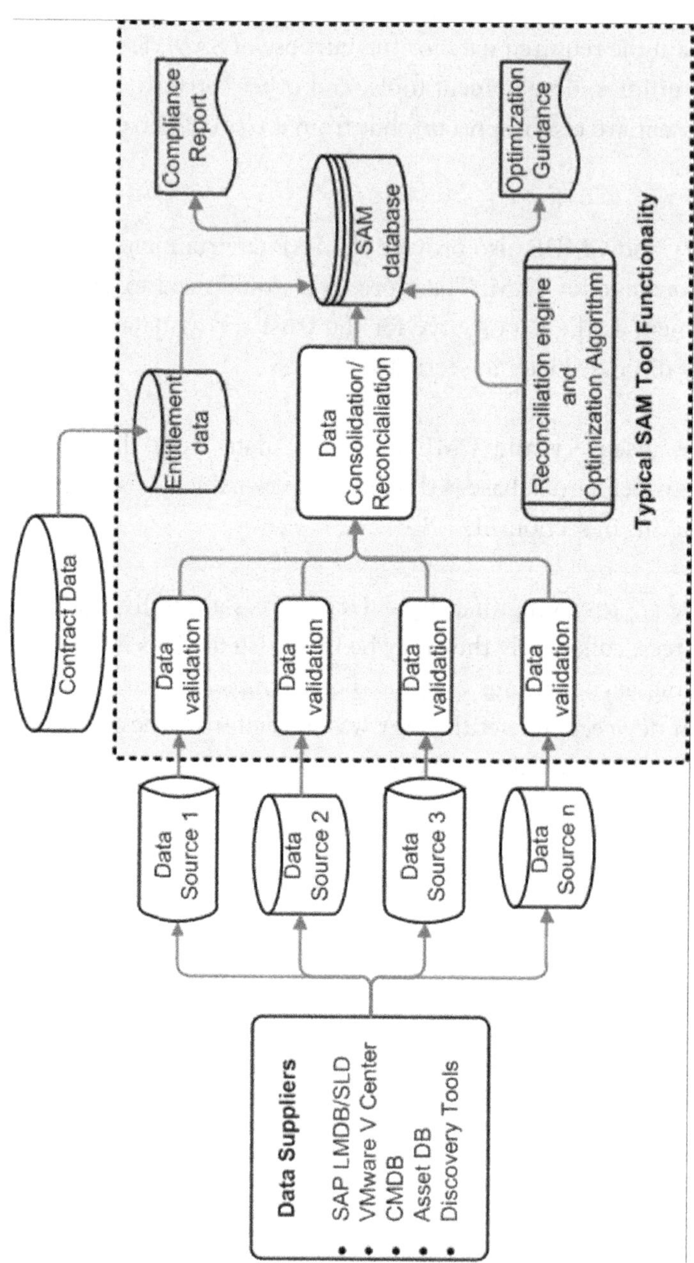

Figure 7. Typical data flow

Therefore, data quality maintenance is one of the integral parts of the SAM. This includes master data maintenance for the SAM system such as a product catalog for normalization.

3.10 Other Processes

In the solution architecture, we have shown one box of "other processes." These are triggered by the action items coming out of the analysis of the reports. Several of these are covered under the security and controls, and there could be many more examples, such as these:

1. Termination of a contract if the software is not in use
2. Removal of unauthorized software
3. Initiation of license-model change with the vendor
4. Introduction of some new controls of policies
5. Corrective actions for noncompliance
6. And many more

These are the finishing touches to the SAM process without which SAM will lose most of its purpose and value.

4 IMPLEMENTATION APPROACH

The first step of any implementation plan starts with the assessment of the current state. For any journey, we determine where are we and where we want to go. We are assuming that the organizations know the current state of their SAM. We are also assuming that the organizations have vision and strategy in place.

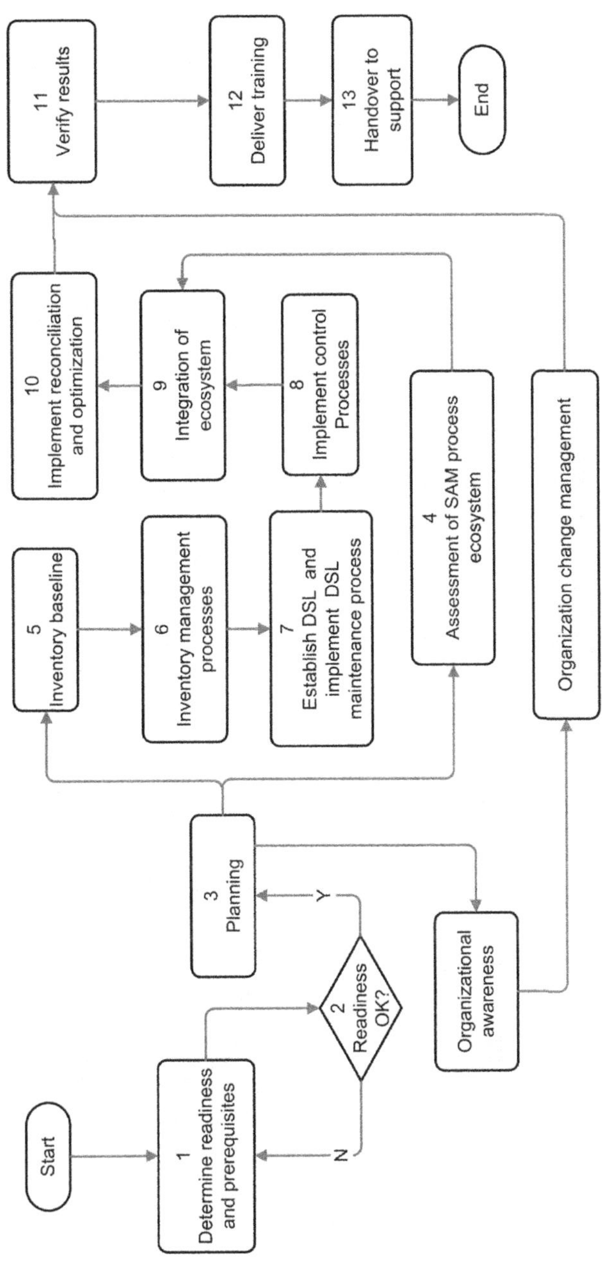

Figure 8. SAM implementation approach

The two boxes "Organizational Awareness" and "Organization Change Management" are nontechnical yet very difficult to do but crucial for the success of the project.

4.1 Readiness Check

There may be very strong reasons to go for a comprehensive SAM, but is your organization ready for it? The purpose of readiness assessment is to help your organization prepare to deal with obstacles that would otherwise delay SAM initiatives. By identifying barriers, your organization can address issues before they escalate to major problems, therefore saving time and increasing the likelihood of successfully implementing SAM.

Executive Sponsorship

SAM projects require participation and cooperation from people across all technical and nontechnical IT groups and business groups such as purchase, vendor management, and so forth. Executive sponsorship is one of the most important nontechnical aspects of a SAM project. Technical experts in the technical team would surely know how to implement the tools and processes, but rarely is thought given to the people aspect of SAM projects. These people aspects are a significant piece of organization change management (OCM), and no OCM can be successful without executive sponsorship. Besides OCM, commitment on resources and participation is brought by executive sponsorship. So ask the first readiness question: Has sponsorship for the SAM project been committed to at a senior-management or board level?

The good news is that SAM would always be on the radar of executive management, including CFOs, because of compliance requirements and legal risks associated with the unauthorized use of software.

Organizational Awareness

Organizational awareness is the first step of organizational change management. Before you attempt to change people, you should make them aware of what is changing, why it is changing, and when will it change. Think of the following scenarios as examples where people will start complaining after SAM implementation:

1. People cannot download and install any software from the Internet.
2. People had the luxury of MS Project Professional on your laptop only to read .mpp files; now they have to manage with Project Reader only.
3. People cannot buy any software and get reimbursed because the policy has changed.

So ask the second readiness question: Has the profile of SAM been raised within the organization, and is the SAM culture developing?

SAM Vision and Strategy

Vision comes first. If you have a clear vision, you can develop the right strategy. If you develop a strategy without vision, it will fail. The vision would be the statement of the end state of the SAM ecosystem that includes processes, tools, function, and governance. Vision first means you need to create a document describing the desired state you want at the closure of the project. Strategy will then define the direction to get there. This direction could be the top-level plan. The solution architecture described in section 2 could be the statement of the end state. For many organizations it would be very ambitious, so section 5 also presents a scaled-down solution that is good enough for compliance purposes. Therefore, ask the third readiness question: Have the vision and strategy for SAM been documented and agreed upon?

A yes answer to this question means you have taken a decision on the architecture and tool set and a top-level solution design is ready.

Business Case

SAM projects costs money. Business drivers, scope, and financial metrics are the basis for investment in most projects, but SAM has an additional element of legal compliance, which resonates very well with executive management. This does not mean that you do not need a business justification. Sponsors will still need to know the scope and the financial metrics. So ask the fourth readiness question: Has the business case been accepted and approved?

For SAM projects, it is usually not difficult to prepare a good business case. If you only think of compliance as the goal, then you would be good with only a part of the full-process ecosystem that is described in section 3, which offers a holistic solution.

According to Gartner ("The Business Case for Software Asset Management," September 2007) the required investment in SAM is about 3%–5% of the software license cost. This is intriguing because you do not know the correct software costs until you have good SAM. Another data point is that you can save 10%–30% of software cost with a good SAM. You should use both the data points as guiding benchmark to make your investment decision.

Forrester research ("Opportunities in a Growth Market Accelerated by 'the Recession,'" May 2008) suggests that a good SAM can save, on average, compliance cost of ten dollars in software per device and also saves, by virtue of license optimization, about fifty dollars per desktop and three hundred dollars per server. Further, it also finds that there is a saving of 10% in IT support costs in training, research, and productivity improvement.

Budget and Resources

In enterprise IT, the resources are always finite and coping with infinite wants. It is actually a matter of priority where you want to put your resources. In the context of SAM, the output of the last lag (the optimization and compliance) will deliver the real ROI. The resource loading in the project may be very uneven during different phases. For example, in terms of preparation for discovery versus actual discovery, the ratio of efforts could be 80/20. Besides this, SAM is also operation intensive—you need adequate resources beyond the project.

So ask the question: Have the resources for the project as well as operations been committed?

Summary of readiness questions

- Has sponsorship for the SAM project been committed to at a senior-management or board level?
- Has the profile of SAM been raised within the organization, and is the SAM culture developing?
- Have the vision and strategy for SAM been documented and agreed upon?
- Has the business case been accepted and approved?
- Have the resources for the project as well as operations been committed?

4.2 Scope and Planning

Vision and strategy have very much set the direction so you know in which direction to move, and you likely also know how far you need to go. The next question is: What is the next step? The answer lies in planning. Planning is the step where you detail out the program. We consider that box "planning and implementation" in figure 5 represents multiple interlinked projects, and we shall describe each of them.

At the beginning of the project, you must carefully define the scope of SAM. In an ideal world, each and every software and license should be controlled and managed via SAM. But we suggest following the 80/20 rule: 80% of benefits can be achieved by 20% of the products. You may also consider increasing the scope in phases. The basis for phasing could be either the number of products in the scope or the functionality of the solution. For example, you may decide that limiting the scope to selected vendor products like Microsoft, IBM, and Oracle products in Phase 1 will be good enough. Alternatively you may choose only the license-compliance part in Phase 1 and drop things like DSL and security control features. In Phase 2 you can increase the product scope and add DSL as well as security control features. A license-compliance report is the best quick win you should aim for. The most important tip for deciding the scope is this: Do not get tempted to scope based on tool capabilities alone. Tools are powerful and can do great things, but there are many things that people and processes have to do that are even more complex and demanding. After you have agreed on the scope in terms of products and functionality, you will be able to prepare the project plan and the resource plan.

1. Products in scope
2. Establish project plan and resource plan
3. Establish RACI (responsible, accountable, consulted and informed)
4. SAM planning
    a. Establish SAM policies
    b. Communicate and institutionalize policy
    c. Implement controls
    d. Establish techniques for discovery of policy breaches
    e. Define and implement risk mitigation plan

4.3 Inventory Baseline

You must create an inventory baseline of all installed software in scope. Depending upon the tool set in your architecture, you will have multiple options for where to build the inventory database. These options include the following:

- Your ITSM system
- Your asset management system (you might have a separate one)
- Underlying database of the discovery tool

Many ITSM systems do not differentiate the asset DB and CMDB and maintain one single database. We prefer to have asset DB and CMDB separate. CMDB is a complex database, but the configuration-management process is simple. Asset DB is a simple database, but asset management is a complex process. By combining CMDB and asset DB, you will end up having a complex database as well as a complex process. It is better to deal with one complexity at a time. In any case, you will be creating a new database or working on an existing database to achieve the accuracy and completeness of the inventory baseline. Since software runs on the hardware and license metrics accounts for the hardware, you will also be required to include hardware in the inventory baseline.

If you have decided to use your CMDB as a data provider for SAM, you must make an assessment of whether it is designed to serve the purpose of SAM. We believe in most cases the answer is negative for the following reasons:

1. CMDB usually focuses on the production environment, and the goal is to be an information provider for assessing the service impact of a CI. Since development systems are not critical for services, you might have kept them out of CMDB scope by design.
2. The configuration-management process to maintain accuracy is built around the change controls, and development environments are not

in the scope of change control, so even if the data is there, it may not be accurate.

3. End-user devices may not be in CMDB because those are service-consuming systems and not the service-producing system and you build CMDB to hold only the information about the service-producing system.

This will lead to a plan for repurposing CMDB, which may not be a good idea without considering the alternatives.

Usually you will be collecting data from multiple sources beyond discovery if you are building a CMDB and asset DB to serve SAM. Actually the same purpose is completely solved by the discovery data. As we said earlier, the discovery for CMDB is different for than the SAM, and the discovery for SAM is much less complex. A typical exercise will include data collection, data verification, and normalization. The tool will automate most of this. The critical part is the tool capability for software recognition and product catalog for normalization. If you have very limited scope, then you may build your own product catalog.

While creating an inventory baseline, you should be open to nontraditional data sources much beyond discovery tools. All organizations have event monitoring and control tools. These tools hold the data of all the devices they are monitoring. You may consider this as an additional data source. Yet another important data source could be patch-deployment tools. Normally, the reach of discovery should be highest and the discovery of patch-management tools should be the lowest. But incorrect implementation and configuration may cause this assumption to fail. In one environment we observed that a discovery tool was able to discover about 70% of the devices that were monitored by the monitoring tool, and, even more surprising, the patch-deployment tool was able to cover 85% of the devices that were monitored.

4.4 *Inventory Management*

While you are creating the inventory baseline, you should also simultaneously develop the inventory-management process. These are the processes to keep the inventory up to date in the operation. If you have a strong request fulfillment process, you are in a very good state. The request for deployment of new software will usually come through request fulfillment by an end user or through change and release management by business demand. All you need to do is strengthen your demand-management, request-management, change-management, and release-management processes and bring inventory under the control of these processes.

Typical processes for data maintenance should include the clear procedures for the following:

- Add/delete new asset and license
- Add/delete new product
- Modify license model
- Modify existing asset attribute

4.5 *Definitive Software Library Build*

DSL is the library that maintains the authorized copy of all the software in use. DSL not only helps SAM but also reduces operational problems. DSL has two parts. One is the database that will provide the list of all the software with its attributes and the location where the deployable copy of the software resides, and the second part is the storage on the network with a strong access control where this executable software will be stored. Therefore, building a DSL will involve a massive undertaking of collecting the authorized master copies and storing them. Simultaneously, you will build the simple database most probably in the ITSM system, which will provide the information about all the software and its attributes.

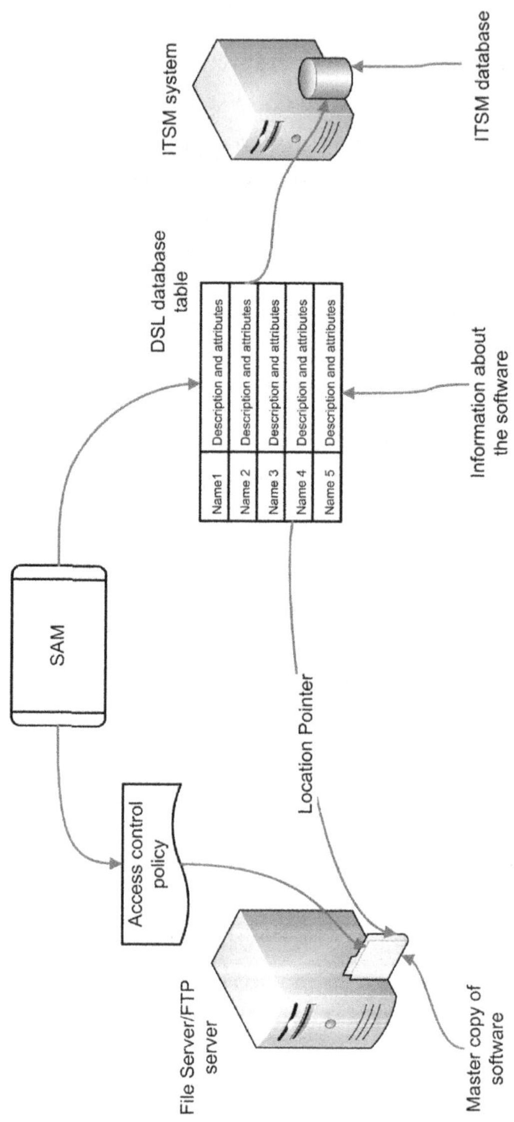

Figure 9. DSL

DSL Database

The DSL database should be built in the ITSM tool to enable easy integration with release-management and demand-management processes. Most of the data in the DSL table will come from CMDB and the product catalog. We expect that the product catalog will include the fields standardized by ISO for SWID tags. If not, it is strongly recommended to include them in the DSL table. Mandatory data elements as defined in section 3.2.2 should also be the mandatory field in the DSL table, and most of the optional data elements described in same section. These fields should be considered for inclusion in DSL fields. In addition, other fields like cost center, release owner, and so forth will come from CMDB and ITSM systems. The location would be one of the mandatory data elements in the DSL table and should include the link where the authorized copy of the software is located.

DSL Baseline

Here is the list of key steps to establish a DSL. The steps are very simple but tedious and time-consuming:

- Identify scope of DSL (list of software items under controls).
- Identify master copy source of each software.
- Collect master copy.
- Establish a network storage.
- Implement access controls.
- Store and secure master copy.
- Collect proof of ownership.
- Develop data model for DSL database.
- Define the taxonomy.

- Define the data elements and populate DSL database.
- Define and implement processes to maintain DSL currency and security.

DSL Controls

The DSL control process will include developing and implementing two things—the access control and the DSL maintenance process.

Typical, the DSL maintenance process will include the following:

1. Adding and removing access to the executable (DSL storage)
2. Adding or modifying the record in the DSL
3. Adding the new versions of authorized software in DSL storage

Release management is one of the control processes. After UAT (user acceptance test) is signed off, the deployment pack of the new version of the software will be deposited in DSL storage, and a DSL entry will be added. The deployment process under the control of change management will pick up the deployment pack from DSL and push it into production. The DSL database is also a place to store the electronic copy of proof of purchase or proof of ownership, in addition to the contract-management database, because many software are procured without contract, such as retail packages of software. This proof of purchase will not be available in the contract-management database.

4.6 Risks and Controls

4.6.1 Typical Risks

There are several entry points that can expose you for litigation. Understand these and establish countermeasures with appropriate policies and processes.

1. **Upgrade licenses:** Many upgrade packs are virtually the whole product but the license is considered legal only if it is installed upon the older version product. Further, the original product on which the upgrade is installed should be licensed.
2. **Academic licenses:** Faculty member are consultants in many organizations and are provided with enterprise-owned laptops to access the enterprise network. A consultant may install a licensed product that he has bought as a faculty member. Although it is fully licensed and legal for personal use, it makes the enterprise noncompliant because the academic version is not allowed to be used for company-owned hardware.
3. **Bundle breaking:** If you receive a bundle of five applications, installation of the entire bundle is OK, but breaking the bundle and installing individual applications on five different computers is a violation of the license term and an instance of piracy although, from technical point of view, you are still using one instance of one application.
4. **Hard-disk loading:** Some organizations use the original image that comes with the hardware, especially the end-user laptop, under certain circumstances (like some special-purpose requirement that may not be met by standard model and OS image), and may receive a trial version for a limited time. If they do not uninstall after the trial-period expiry, it is a violation of license T&C and potential piracy.
5. **Reimaging:** Technicians solve many end-user problems by reimaging the entire system. This is not only an opportunity to bring the system under corporate-approved software and compliance but also a risk when the technician agrees to and installs user-provided software without checking its authenticity.
6. **Nonexecutable software:** Music files and videos are copyrighted material, and the existence of these files on company machines is a potential risk. It is an expensive affair to implement controls and force those controls to eliminate this risk; nonetheless, enterprise IT should recognize

this risk and bring in some practical controls. iTunes, for example, enforces controls to copy music files and video files from iPhones (you can transfer from an iPhone to another registered device, and there is limit on how many devices can be reasonably considered as your personal device and on which transfer is allowed). However, iTunes allows unrestricted copy of photo files taken from an iPhone camera.

4.6.2 SAM Policies

A policy is the statement of rules and guidelines that will tell what you want a task to do. Policies and guidelines are supported by the processes that cover how you will do this task. Some part of the policies is enforced. The guideline part of the policies is usually not enforceable, but rather left to the discretion of the task actor. Enforced policies are a higher level of controls, but everything cannot be enforced. Following are the general SAM policies that should be developed and institutionalized. We believe that all organizations have matured information-security-management processes. CSO (chief security officer) has methods to institutionalize information-security policies. It would be a good idea to learn from those and replicate them in SAM areas.

The following are some of the essential points around which SAM should develop appropriate policies.

1. **Use and misuse of system:** Information security has an established policy; add the SAM relevance into that.
2. **Software selection and evaluation:** The enterprise architecture group might have this already. Review and enhance if required.
3. **Selection of vendors or resellers**: Vendor management would already have this. Review and make it relevant for SAM.
4. **Procurement policy:** Procurement policy exists in all organizations. Review and make it relevant for SAM. Centralize all purchases through a designated authority. Don't permit employees to buy

software directly or charge it to their expense accounts. Buy only from approved vendors.

5. **Use of personal software:** Disallow use of personal software on enterprise-owned machines.
6. **Use of shareware and freeware:** Clarify what is permissible and what is not.
7. **Software request:** Ensure the software being requested is on the approved list of supported software.
8. **Software approval:** Ensure all software purchase requests are recorded and approved.
9. **Downloading of software:** Ensure that even a legal software cannot be downloaded from the Internet by employees without special approval.
10. **Copying of software:** Use the copying terms and condition of original manufactures. They allow it for some purpose.
11. **Protection of organization's IP:** Don't permit employees to download peer-to-peer client software that may be used for trading copyrighted works.
12. **Software-receiving policy:** Get original user materials such as licenses and receipts for each purchase.

Policies Need Maintenance

Processes and policies (as the component of processes) are like software and thus need maintenance. We have provided a detailed concept of process maintenance in our book *Process Excellence for IT Operations.*

Because of the dynamic nature of business, policies keep changing. For example, when a software vendor changes its terms in the contract, you may need to review and if required amend the SAM policies. For example, if the device-based license term becomes enterprise or site license, you will remove the approval process for individual instance installation. You may, from time to time, introduce new policies or change existing policies regarding approvals. For example, you may like to reduce the consumption of licenses because of increased prices and will add a business-justification step in the software-installation process.

4.6.3 General Controls

These are not all but a few very common control processes that you should consider to be in place, at minimum.

Prevention of Installation of Unauthorized Software

A company can force an employee to run all of its corporate applications inside a virtual machine on the computer, which seals company information off from everything else. This will shift the burden on centralized maintenance, but this may not be possible for many corporations, especially in the new world.

You can also implement a control in the request process by building the IT-approved software catalog and forcing selection only from the approved catalog. But what about software obtained from unauthorized sources?

It is very easy to prevent the installation of unauthorized software by preventing administrative rights on the desktop. It would be impossible not to provide administrative access to an employee working with a company laptop. Even a desktop user without administrative rights can download and use nonexecutable software that comes under copyright protection. Internet access is the standard part of every workplace, as Internet is treated as a necessary research tool for every kind of work, so you cannot block Internet access (other than blocking access to named sites).

Thus, this control should largely be achieved by education and institutionalization of policies and creating a culture of social responsibilities, like security management says—Security is everyone's responsibility.

Detection and Removal of Unauthorized Software

If you cannot enforce the prevention of unauthorized software installation, you can at least detect and remove it. Configuration-monitoring tools are widely available for this job. Advanced and expensive tools allow real-time detection and alerting. Real-time detection may not be worth its cost in all environments. Rather than for compliance purpose, real-time monitoring is more useful and business justified for critical application infrastructure to maintain the stability of the environment and to improve the services and reduce the business impact. For compliance purposes, use a periodic process of benchmarking the "golden" configuration with the actual configuration and detecting the unauthorized software. If your change-management process is well designed, there will be a process of detecting unauthorized changes. Unauthorized software can be detected by this process. However, this will still not be sufficient because, from a license-management and compliance perspective, nonproduction systems are in scope, and the change-management process does not address that. Therefore, you must establish and operate an audit process for this purpose.

Harvesting of Unused Licenses

There are several reasons that a software may be installed but not in use. In the scenarios that follow, you would uninstall and harvest:

1. Installed software is part of bundle that you purchased, and you cannot break it. This will not impact you, either from a compliance perspective of from a financial perspective. You may choose to analyze if the bundle is worth its value if you have a large number of such instances. This is not a candidate for harvesting. You will not uninstall it either.

2. Installed software is part of a bundle that you received as trial software. This is a tricky situation. It does not affect you financially but may affect you from a compliance perspective, depending upon the trial-software licensing terms. There are multiple scenarios within this scenario:

   a. If the trial software was activated and then never used or was not activated at all

   b. If the trial software does not need activation and gets installed and activated as a part of the bundle installation

   c. Regardless of installation, the resident file is deemed a license liability as per the manufacturer's term

These are candidates for uninstalling but not for harvesting.

3. Software was installed for a user who changed his role and no longer requires this software. These are the candidates for harvesting. You will uninstall and harvest the license. If you have a good account-management process, or ITIL access-management process, you should be able to do this proactively because the role change will also trigger the access control and new account creation in another system. You can check, at that time, if there is any need to retain the existing software. In fact, you can have a verification process on every software-install process that will reverify the existing software installed and also revalidate the need.

4. Finally, you may have the cases where the software was installed without any need. This is a weakness of the software-install process or the

approval process within that. If you have a good qualification process, you will install the software on a need basis and it will be in use. This is the candidate for uninstall and harvest.

Reclamation of Software against Disposed Hardware

Hardware-asset retire and disposal is an essential part of every hardware-management process. We also have informal or ad hoc reclamation of certain spare parts from retired systems. A simple step of adding the license-reclaiming step would deliver a significant cost benefit. This is a financial gain rather than a compliance need.

Overuse of Licenses

Not all overuse cases require purchases of additional license. The first attempt should be made for looking at an alternate option that can be determined by optimization methods.

Change and Release management: The most fundamental controls

A comprehensive change and release management process can significantly support the license compliance. All organizations do have some level of controls in change management process to manage the risk of disruption or interruption to the business. A SAM point of view in the risk assessment and approval, or the checklist before change implementation is the simplistic approach and should not be perceived as the bureaucracy. For example, if you are upgrading the CPU on a server, you may be going out of compliance if the license is linked to the CPU power, or if you are adding a node to a cluster, then you have to consider the license T &C.

Similarly, for release management, when you are creating the deployment pack, you need to have the SAM view on the license compliance aspect of the whole deployment pack. One component of a release pack may push you out of compliance

4.7 Internal SAM Ecosystem Integration

The SAM system consists of multiple process and tools and functions. It will be a mini project by itself to integrate all of it together. Although most people think of tool integration, in reality it is process integration that is realized by integration of underlying tools. Typical integration examples are these:

1. Integration of the discovery tool with the inventory-management tool under the control of reconciliation
2. Integration of the SR (service request aka request fulfillment) process with inventory management
3. Integration of release with DSL

In addition to process and tools, you will also be required to do function integration and establish operation integration roles and assign those roles to the right people. These people will coordinate and facilitate collaboration for the purpose of SAM. See the following examples:

- Interface with demand management
- Interface with release management
- Interface with procurement management
- Interface with contract management

Closed-Loop Ecosystem Illustration for SAM

Figure 10 is a depiction of a closed-loop process ecosystem in the context of SAM. Anything and everything that we do in an enterprise IT can be traced back to one of the three points of origin: first, an end user has some need or trouble that needs to be fulfilled or resolved; second, the business has some demand for adding a new service or modifying an existing service; or third, a configuration item in the environment that is contributing to the production of a service is getting unhealthy. We will illustrate how this process ecosystem works in the context of SAM.

One of the triggers for the SAM process ecosystem is an end user requesting a software install. When he initiates a request, the request-fulfillment process will start. SAM has enforced one rule at this point, which is that the user can choose from the approved list of software that is built and published under the control of SAM. SAM will also dictate the policies to the request-fulfillment process for qualification and approval of the request. SAM will also provide request-management access to DSL to install the software for the end user by the fulfillment task of request management. At this point, SAM will also update its database of license count. In case the licenses are not available or the entitlement limit has been reached, SAM will ask request management to hold the installation and trigger the procurement-management process, which will procure under the contract and issue the purchase order. SAM will receive the software and then trigger the task in request fulfillment to install the software. Successful installation by the task of request management will send the confirmation to SAM that will close the record for that license.

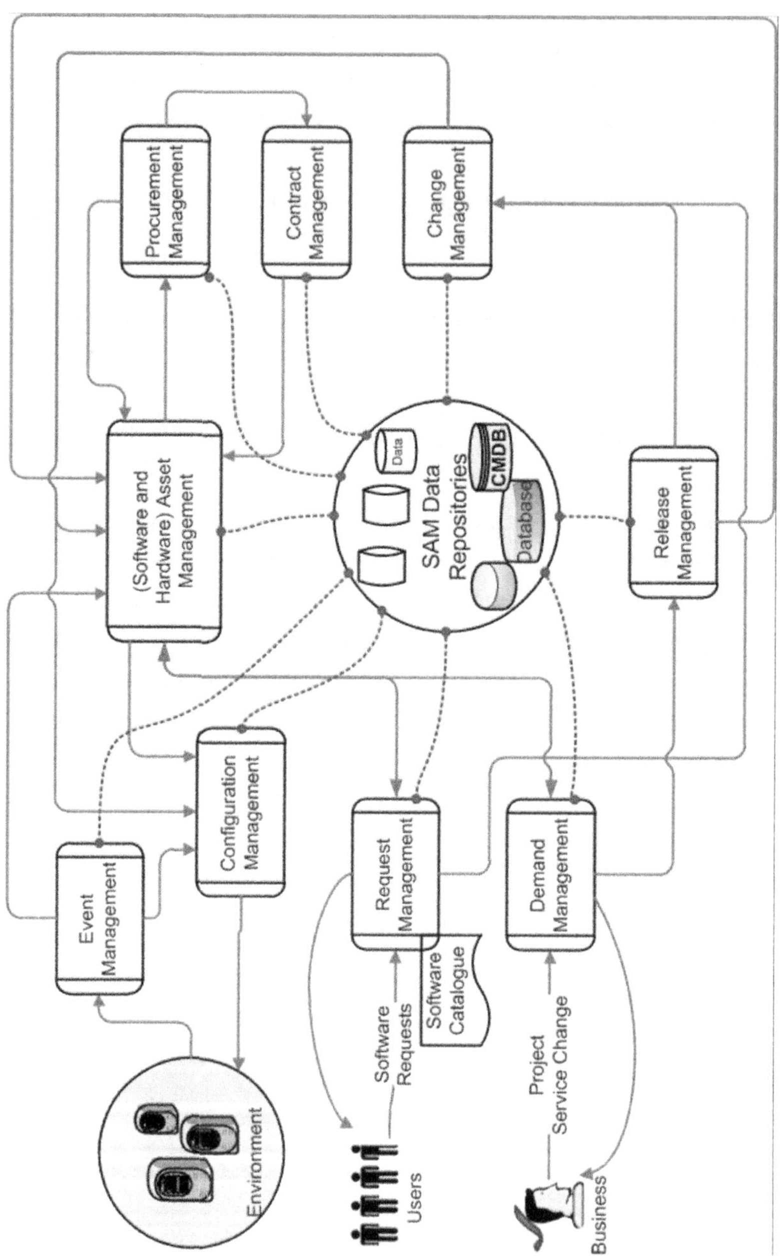

Figure 10. Closed-loop process ecosystem

The second example is the origination from business that will initiate a demand that may translate into the new software requirement and licensing. Demand management will trigger SAM, and the similar process as we discussed for request management will repeat. The only difference here is that the software selection and qualification will happen after the demand has been placed, unlike the enforcement of selection through the software catalog of request management. For fulfilling of all demand originated from the business, release management will be triggered. Release management will deposit the deployment pack in DSL that will be deployed by change management. Release management will interact with SAM for depositing software in DSL. Change management will also interact with SAM for access to the DSL. A successful deployment will send confirmation to SAM for record updates.

The third example is about monitoring and managing the software inventory in the environment. Configuration management will maintain the accuracy and currency of inventory and CMDB and the relationship of all hardware and software. Configuration management uses discovery and reconciliation tools. SAM governs configuration management and accounts for the controls to be imposed on configuration management resulting from the triggers from other processes—namely, request, demand, change, and release. Event management will detect the deviations and trigger configuration management for correction. It will also inform SAM for other control actions. The entire process ecosystem will share SAM data repositories, which include CMDB and inventories.

4.8 Reconciliation and Optimization

Once you have an inventory baseline with normalized data, you will need to collect the entitlement data. Entitlement data is what you have purchased and have a right to use. Your purchase system will supply this data. You will be required to do lot of manual data entry here. When your entitlement data is available you can run the reconciliation. Reconciliation engines are an integral part of SAM tools. Mature products provide reconciliation capability of many complex license models. The output of this reconciliation is primarily the compliance report. In addition, the report will also provide the usage pattern and many clues for optimization. At this point, based on this report, you will trigger optimization actions and other kinds of actions.

- Configuring and testing reconciliation engine
- Running and testing report
- Implementing optimization methods

4.9 Assessment of Existing Processes

Assessment of SAM process ecosystem: While you are pursuing steps mentioned in box 5, 6, 7 and 8 as shown in figure 8, you will also trigger another project of SAM ecosystem assessment, that is mentioned in box 4. This will study the current state of all the ecosystem individual processes and identify the gaps. These gaps will feed into the integration of the ecosystem. Assessment comprises three phases: work-information collection, information review and validation, and finally the analysis and conclusion.

Information Collection

The key objective of this phase will be to gather the information regarding services and methods that exists in documented and undocumented form. Information-collection methods will include workshop, interviews and soft and hard copy of document gathering.

Information Review

The key objective of this phase is to review the consolidated information and prepare for the gap analysis. During this phase you will review and consolidate all information gathered thus far.

Information validation is a part of information review and includes checking the validity of information collected. This includes checking for consistency, clarity, and contradictions among the different sources of information. You may seek further clarifications to remove the inconsistencies that were determined in the earlier step.

Information Analysis

The key objective of this phase is to identify gaps and determine the optimal method to plug in those gaps.

4.10 Organization Change Management

Organization change management is a totally nontechnical project led by nontechnical people to ensure that people are aware and educated and ready to adapt to the new process. We are not experts in this subject and do not intend to provide any guidance on OCM. The purpose of including this section is to bring awareness that all tools, technologies, processes, policies, organization structure, roles, and so forth will fail to deliver the desired outcome if this aspect is not considered and addressed. Experts outside IT should drive OCM.

From the perspective of SAM solution implementation and operation, training is one of the components of OCM. The solution should identify the roles and identify the persons to whom those roles will be mapped. If they have some role to play in the operation of the SAM process, the training should be delivered in time.

4.11 SAM in Operation

This section briefs the operational activities for software asset management.

1. **Tool and process maintenance:** The activities related to tools administration, support, and maintenance are very well understood. Most often, it is the process that breaks down while the tools work perfectly. Process breakdown or process failure often give an illusion of tool failure. Therefore, process maintenance should be a part of standard operations. We have given adequate explanation of process maintenance in our book *Process Excellence for IT Operations.*

2. **Integration maintenance:** The integrated tool set will have several integrations and usually is a part of the tool maintenance, but we are listing it as a separate point because of the emphasis on looking at it as process integration as well.

3. **Process master data maintenance:** While we are drowned in a lot of transaction data in the ITSM system, we ignore the importance of process master data maintenance. Master data includes the taxonomies, profiles, and tool-configuration data and is crucial for any process operation.

4. **Inventory maintenance using implemented processes:** Mind the words "using implemented processes." SAM operations are responsible for maintaining the inventory, but we mean that good processes

should be in place and that it should be a matter of operating those processes.

5. **Regular reconciliation and optimization:** This is the job that delivers the most value. At regular periods you should reconcile and optimize to maintain compliance and keep it cost-effective as well.
6. **Actions on compliance reports:** Compliance reports may lead to several actions such as uninstallation, procurement, or changing the license model. In addition to that, regular audits would also lead to remedial actions. SAM would assume the operational ownership for these actionable items and either perform the actions within its control process or get it done through other processes.

4.11.1 Roles within the SAM Function

Roles are defined for the purpose of segregation of duties and do not translate into the head count. A person can take more than one role if there is no conflict of interest, and one role can be mapped to multiple persons if the volume of work demands.

SAM Process Owner

The process owner is the person who owns the process as an asset. Ownership is tied with accountability for the result that is expected from the process. This means that the process owner owns all the components of the process—he or she signs off on the process document and policies. If a process needs to be changed, the process owner must approve that change. He or she is accountable to keep the process aligned with business needs. The process owner usually appoints a process manager to monitor and maintain the process.

SAM Process Manager

A process manager is the administrator of the process who monitors and maintains the performance of the process. The process manager is responsible for the functionality of the process, while the process owner is accountable for the result of the process.

The process manager does not execute the process tasks but audits the tasks' execution, policy, and compliance. He or she also measures the internal KPIs (key performance indicators) of the process to determine the health condition of the process. Continual process improvement is the extended responsibility of the process manager. When determining an improvement opportunity that requires policy or workflow change, a process manager obtains the approval of the process manager to implement it.

Hardware Asset and Inventory Manager

The job of the hardware asset and inventory manager is to keep the inventory data current and track every asset through the life cycle. This includes asset tagging, issuing for build and deployment, and disposal after decommissioning. The process owner and process manager will enable the asset manager to ensure that the processes are designed for the purpose of life-cycle tracking.

Software Asset Manager and Librarian

The software asset manager does the same job but for the software assets. That means he is the custodian of DSL and media.

SAM Operation and Compliance Manager

The compliance manager is responsible for running the compliance report and ensuring compliance and takes ownership of the actions required for compliance and optimization.

4.11.2 SAM Supporting Roles

In addition to the mainstream SAM roles, supporting roles are required for a successful SAM.

The architecture and technology advisory group will be responsible for software selection and standardization for all the software.

Vendor management will be responsible for the contract and vendor management.

Other process owners and managers are expected to maintain and manage the supporting processes and tools in the ecosystem.

4.12 SAM for the Private Cloud

The principles of SAM would remain the same in case of a private cloud or even when extended to a public cloud. SAM governs the enterprise liability of managing the licenses regardless of deployment technology. However, there are certain considerations around entitlements of where these licenses can be deployed that govern the same. In case of the private cloud, it becomes very important to manage licensing in a virtualized environment, which is what most of the private-cloud deployments are built on. Also as the private-cloud deployments mostly are done via a self-service portal with a defined catalog, it can be easier to manage consumption and harvesting of licenses as the environment is governed as a resource pool. Integration of the cloud platform with the SAM platform is essential to achieve the same.

5 ALTERNATIVE SOLUTION

All organizations may not find cost justifications for the comprehensive SAM solution as described earlier. For that purpose we are presenting an alternative and scaled-down solution.

5.1 Solution Overview

Figure 11 provides the overview of an alternative solution.

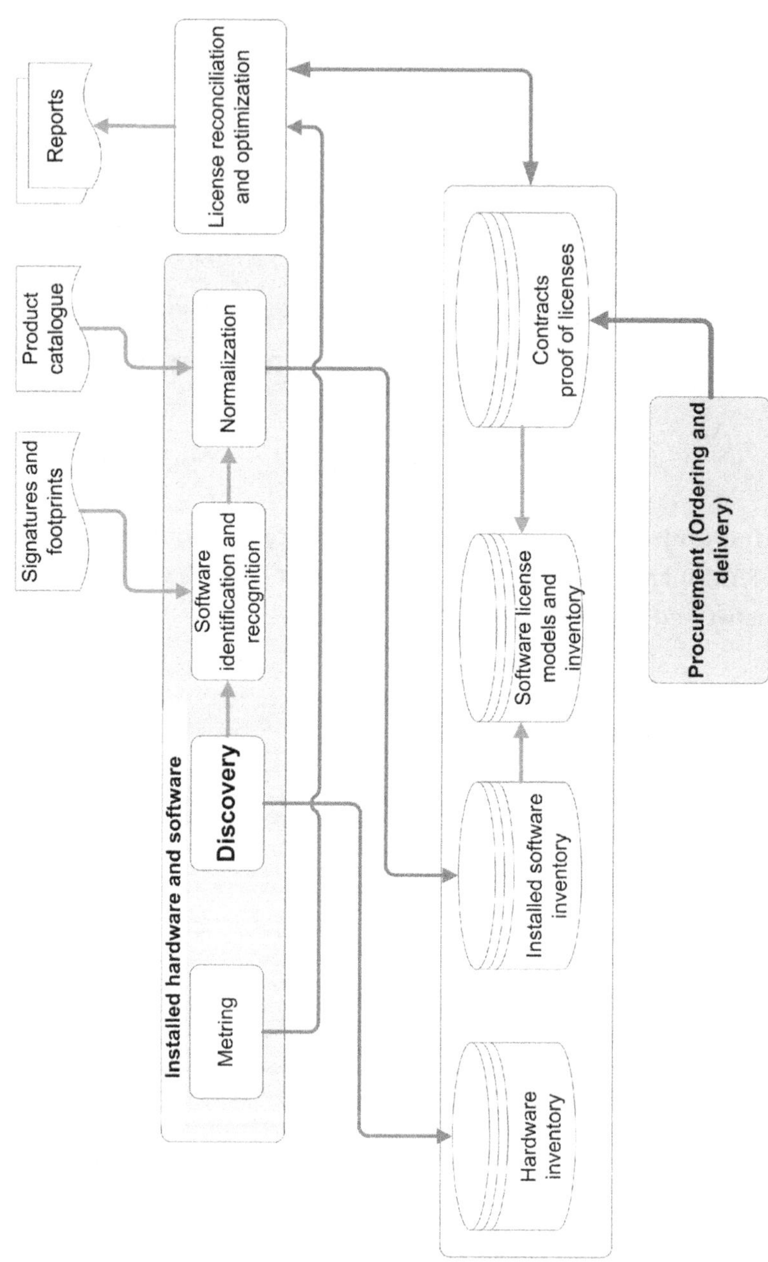

Figure 11. Basic license management

5.1.1 Goal of Alternative Solution

The base solution is independent of any ITSM solution and out of the service-management ecosystem. It focuses on license-compliance management and usage optimization. The basic principle is to regularly run discovery and obtain other data and then reconcile with the entitlements and produce a report.

In most of the organization, compliance-report filing happens annually. All you need to do is run discovery, assess the compliance, and then either uninstall the overuse licenses or purchase the additional license and then after these actions rerun the discovery and verify the compliance. Data flow, as shown in Figure 7 can also be viewed as the alternate view of this solution.

5.1.2 Value of the Alternate Solution

There are two major expectations from any SAM solution—the compliance report and the cost-reduction or license-cost optimization. The alternate solution proposed here delivers both. However, it does not prescribe the remedial measures if the report points to noncompliance. Somebody has to determine the best remedial action and then act as well. The comprehensive solution includes this. Besides this, the alternate solution does not talk about the controls to prevent noncompliance while the comprehensive solution addresses that also.

The alternate solution is like an unstable system, where you periodically identify and fix the instability but do not eliminate the cause of instability. In many business cases, it is viable to live with the alternate solution.

5.1.3 Implementation of Alternate solution (Project)

Implementation will deal with deploying the tools, integration of the tools and configuring the tools with foundation data. It is like setting up the manufacturing machinery for production that will take the raw material, process the raw material and deliver the finished goods.

The second part of the project would be to select a few vendors and onboard them on the solution platform. On boarding includes

7. Collecting Entitlement Data such as contracts and purchase data for specific vendor (proof of purchase, license certificates, License Modeling etc.)
8. Collecting/discovering the usage data
9. Normalizing the data
10. Signature creation for specific vendor
11. Processing and determining the effective license position

This is equivalent to run the production machinery with sample production batch and demonstrate the finished goods (ELP) are produced as required.

During the onboarding process, SAM operation team should also be training

5.1.4 Operation of Alternate solution

Onboarding more vendors and produce the ELP for each vendor is the operation job. Although delivering ELP report is definitely a primary job of operation team, they will also be expected to consult or implement the remedial actions if ELP is pointing to non compliance status.

6 ASSESSMENT AND AUDITS

Assessment and audit are two different mechanisms to assure the success of SAM on an ongoing basis. Assessment targets the SAM processes, SAM tools and SAM function that these elements are designed according to best practice and can achieve the SAM goals effectively and efficiently. Audit verifies that the results are produced as desired. Assessment is checking the method, and audit is verifying the result. Both can lead to gap analysis and correction or improvements.

6.1 Assessment

Assessments are the formal mechanisms for comparing operational practice improvement to the performance standards for the purpose of measuring improved process/tool capability and/or to identify potential shortcomings that could be addressed. Just by conducting a formal assessment, an organization is demonstrating a significant level of commitment to improvement. Assessments involve real costs, staff time, and management promotion. Organizations need to be more than just involved in an assessment; they need to be committed to improvement.

Assessments can provide an objective perspective of the current operational process state compared to a standard maturity model and a process framework. Through a thorough assessment, an accurate determination of any process gaps can be quickly completed, recommendations put forward, and action steps planned. A well-planned and well-conducted assessment is a repeatable process. Thus the assessment is a useful management process in measuring progress over time and in establishing improvement targets or objectives.

It would be a good idea to conduct at least an annual assessment of SAM processes and tools to keep the SAM system fit for purpose and fit for use.

6.2 *Audit*

While the assessment is about the system, the processes, and the function for its capability and/or maturity to deliver the desired result, the audit is the verification of the result itself.

Internal Audit or External Audit

An internal or external audit is a close scrutiny of the data sources and the compliance report for authenticity and validity. It can be done by an internal person in the organization outside the SAM organization or by an external consultant. The audit is complementary to the assessment, and both together completely ensure that the method is right, the required inputs are right, and thus the outcome is right as well.

Forced Audit

A forced audit is the last resort and is equivalent to the last battle of the war where the consumer company is sure to lose. It is a rare situation that will not occur unless the victim company is on a suicidal business path. The software vendor forces the audit on the customer company and is extremely rigorous. The key things in the audits are the following:

1. Verify the number of systems with locations that can hold or can deliver a copyrighted product. For example, a desktop connected to a server in the network makes both devices under the scrutiny and audit. You must have accurate and complete documentation of each system and location.
2. Account and verify which of the enforcer's products are present on each of the systems.
3. Minutely examine the paperwork of where you purchased each product. This minute examination is beyond the comprehension of many people. We rely on simple workable receipts, but a determined enforcer may deny that workable receipt. It is as if your account department is seeking the accurate address of start, accurate address of destination, time of start, time of end, taxi number, date of journey, driver's signature, driver/transport company's contact/address, and so on when you submit a taxi-ride claim for official business.
4. Minutely observe the authenticity of the document itself. Counterfeit products or documents are difficult to identify by users but can easily be identified by auditors.
5. Minutely apply the terms of the license. For example, if you have an upgrade license, you will be required to produce an accurate and completely documented upgrade path documented with a verifiable trace to the original product.

The forced audit demands that, after the search warrant is served for the audit, the company should cease all computers-related activities until the audit is complete. And usually the audit will take days or weeks. This means you must close your business, as these days it is impossible to do any business without computers.

7 SPECIAL CONSIDERATIONS

7.1 SAM in Virtual Environments

While server virtualization results in saving power and maintenance costs, it most likely will not save license costs. You may find it very convenient to create copies of a virtual machine in seconds, but this duplicated virtual machine is subject to all the license terms of the software that is running on it.

Three popular licensing models are generally available, and each has its own problem.

1. Device-specific software license models tie the software license to a particular device and may have special condition for movement from one physical host to another. That means that the dynamic load balancing on the hypervisor layer can cause a noncompliance situation.
2. Processor-based software license models require details of the physical processor in order to determine license compliance, but on a virtual machine the hardware details are often hidden by the hypervisor.
3. Virtual machines per host-software license rules allow the software to run on a certain number of virtual machines for each physical machine with a valid license.

Let us illustrate this in the context of Microsoft Windows Server. You need licenses for the maximum number of virtual machine instances running on a server at any point of time. You may create and store as many instances of a server as you want without requiring any additional license.

Windows Server OS licensing is per socket. So if you run a Windows Server OS on a physical machine with two sockets, you need 1 license of Windows Server 2012 R2 standard or Data Center editions. Similarly, if you run a Windows Server OS on a physical machine with four sockets, you need 2 licenses of Windows Server 2012 R2 standard or Data Center editions. This is regardless of the number of cores, or hyper-threading.

Windows Server 2012 R2 Standard grants two Server OS licenses (virtualization rights) for virtual machines. Data Center Edition grants unlimited Server OS licenses. The magic number is ten VMs. If you plan on running ten or more VMs on a host, Data Center Edition makes economical sense. There is another consideration. You may move running instances between licensed servers without requiring additional licenses provided you do not exceed the maximum number of instances each server is licensed to run. In such a scenario, a Data Center Edition license would be a risk-free choice.

Summary

1. You need to account for the licensing terms and conditions for the virtual environment.
2. You should have adequate instrumentation in your metering system.
3. Your license-reconciliation and license-optimization engine in your tool should be capable of handling these license models.

7.2 *SAM for the SAP Environment*

There are two reasons to discuss this point in a separate section. First, the widespread presence of SAP in enterprise IT makes it an important point, and second, trustworthy data in the SAP environment is sourced in a different way.

The SAP licensing model is one of the most complex and confusing as well as generally baffling. While many software vendors establish the license metrics based on number of active and inactive users, or by considering the number of servers and CPUs and the capacity of CPUs, SAP defines licenses according to usage, and the measurement of usage is not defined unambiguously, which is a source of confusion. SAP also uses the term "named users" differently. It is more near to role-based names. For example, there are no real names behind named users—in addition, a named user can have multiple usernames in different systems. SAP license usage is based on "named users." Customers buy various types of "named users" from SAP, such as: professional named users, limited professional named users, employee named users, and so forth. Each "named user" may have a real username attached to it at any given point in time. Switching of the named user from one actual user to another actual user is allowed and is usually required when an employee leaves the company and another joins. There is a lot of complexity in classifying the users.

Trustworthy Data for the SAP Environment

Standard discovery methods and tools as discussed earlier will not be applicable for the SAM environment. Although all the discovery tools have the capability to discover SAP applications, the complex data required for license reconciliation may not be available from discovery tools. The good news is that you do not have to reinvent the wheel for obtaining the trustworthy data for the SAP environment. SLD, system landscape directory, is the data repository equivalent to CMDB in the SAP environment that is used by the SAP Solution Manager for the trustworthy data that will serve the purpose of SAM also. In SAP Solution Manager 7.1, landscape management database (LMDB) has been introduced, which in most scenarios replaces the local SLD (system landscape directory) as the supplier of system data. LMDB, besides the name resonating with CMDB, also used DMTF's (distributed management task force) popular data model CIM (common information model). SAP provides two agents to collect and maintain data in SLD/LMDB:

1. Host agents gather information about the host's operating system.
2. Diagnostics agents (old name SMD agent) gather information of the managed application on the host systems.

Most of the landscape data application is already sent by the managed-application systems to the SLD and from there synchronized to the LMDB. In some cases this data is enriched by data that has been collected by agents and written directly to the CIM-model-based LMDB. Besides, both agent types work together in the data-collection process and provide the following kinds of data that are external to the SAP landscape:

1. OS discovery provides details about the operating system.
2. DB discovery provides details about installed database software(s).
3. MS discovery provides details about Microsoft Internet Information Services on Microsoft operating systems.

Besides the more static landscape information, some functionality of the SAP Solution Manager may also rely on configuration data, which may change over time, to be used for root-cause analysis. Another usage of agents is to collect monitoring data on the OS level as well as on the application system level from the agent host.

Metering, Compliance Reporting, and Optimization

Once you have the trustworthy data, the next step is the data analysis and reporting. The LMDB/SLD in fact provides all the data to apply the license metric and reconcile with entitlements. The complexity of reconcilement is inevitable. Many SAM tools have reconciliation engines, but not all support complex licensing metrics like SAP has. You may have to do lot of manual work supported by an Excel-based homegrown tool.

Further complexity is about optimization. User classification is the key for cost optimization because the cost difference is huge between the professional named user license and the employee named user license. In order to deal with the complexities in the SAP licensing model, many organizations, on their own, have developed a number of informal methods for classifying users and assigning them appropriate SAP license types. Although these methods are simpler and more logical than the strict SAP definitions, their implementation requires the expenditure of significant organizational resources. Automated tools are available that enable organizations to quickly and easily manage their SAP licenses and saving costs.

7.3 Merger and Acquisitions Considerations for SAM

Merger and acquisition is a complex business scenario. Merger of two companies also leads to merger of two enterprise ITs at all levels and is driven by application portfolio merger. SAM is one very small piece of a holistic IT merger. We have presented solution architecture for the holistic SAM. We believe this architecture can be used as the end-state architecture in any enterprise IT and therefore could become the reference architecture of a unified IT. What need to be merged further are these:

1. **Tool optimization in this architecture:** The unified company would want to eliminate the duplicate or redundant tools. For example, HP's

ITSM tool HPSM (HP service manager) can replace BMC Remedy, or BMC Remedy can replace HPSM.

2. **Tweak and optimize to one set of processes and policies:** For example, develop a single process and policy on license requisition/software install.
3. **Create a unified function and roles:** For example a single SAM owner in unified SAM.
4. **Data merger:** Instead of merging the two SAM data sources, you are more likely to create a new trustworthy data source because there might be two different license models for the same vendor software and because of different license metrics. The data may not provide the metering information required for both.

We believe IT has much to learn from business in order to have a business perspective of a merger that drives an IT merger. Let me take an example of what HR does in a merger.

1. Integrate policies and programs from both companies.
2. Process retention, compensation, and benefits packages.
3. Identify key talents and expertise.
4. Advise leadership on organization capability.
5. Recognize customs, symbols, language, and ceremonies needed for cultural assimilation.
6. Design new performance and reward systems.
7. Create communication strategies.
8. Educate organization on what to expect and on new skills.

The entire focus is for unified business architecture and the processes and functions. We would recommend the same approach for IT as well.

7.4 Open Source and SAM

"Open source" is a broad term used to define software that is being developed and supported by communities and individual users and that is governed by different open-source initiatives. The popular ones are GPL (General Public License), Apache License, and Free Software Foundation (FSF). There are also many commercial software vendors who provide open-source components of their code to the community. GITHUB is a popular repository that is used by open-source communities to distribute the software.

There are enterprise software companies whose entire offerings are built on the foundation of open source, like Redhat, Novell Software, Chef, Docker, Puppet Labs, and so on. Many cloud service providers for IaaS and PaaS use extensive open source, and it is one of the most popular mechanisms to consume open-source-based services.

There are more challenges of infringement, liabilities that can be inherited by using open source, so it is important for the enterprise to ensure that correct contractual provisions are made when acquiring software products that have embedded open-source components. Software license management still remains applicable in open-source software when deployed in the enterprise.

8 OUTSOURCING SAM

There are two parts of SAM that can be outsourced:

1. Build SAM
2. Operate SAM

The build part includes the design and implementation of processes, tools, and function to run the SAM. The build part is a finite project. Outsourcing could be tricky if you are building a comprehensive SAM solution as described in section 3, because this solution is comprehensively integrated with the mainstream ITSM system and the scope management for the build SAM project could be very difficult. If you are intending to go for the comprehensive solution and want to outsource, the first recommended step is the assessment and gap analysis between the existing state of SAM as well as ITSM and the target state of the comprehensive solution. With the gap report, you should develop a strategy to achieve the end state, and the outsourcing plan can be derived from that strategy.

If you are opting for the alternate solution as described in section 6, the outsourcing is quite simple and easy to outsource because it is an independent project without any touch points with existing ITSM system.

Activities and roles that can be outsourced for SAM operations are given in section 4.11, but these will vary depending upon the kind of solution you build. When it comes to the outsourcing of the operations, you would require establishing the SLAs (service level agreements), and for that you will be required to define several KPIs. The KPI definitions would depend upon the type of solution. Asset DB accuracy and completeness would be among the most important KPIs. For a comprehensive solution, the additional KPIs would be derived from ITSM processes KPIs.

There is tendency to price the outsourcing service based on the outcome or the result. For this purpose, the clause of noncompliance penalties could be an important bone of contention between the service provider and the customer. If you were opting for the solution described in section 6, it would be impossible for the service provider to agree to the penalty clause. If you were opting for the holistic solution as described in section 3, service providers have controls to prevent noncompliance. However, the terms and conditions of the licenses are so complex that the controls would rarely be foolproof. Under these realistic considerations, the service providers would not agree for the noncompliance penalty, and the customer would bear the risk of noncompliance.

11 APPENDIX 1: SAMPLE TOOL SET

This table lists some of the common tools in the holistic solution architecture. The intention is not to recommend the tool, nor to claim that this is the definitive list. We just want to make readers familiar with distinctive functionality tools.

Functional Bloc in the Architecture	Tool Examples
Asset management	Asset management within IBM Smart Cloud Control Desk CA IT Asset Management HP Asset management ServiceNow—asset management within ITSM BMC Remedy asset management within ITSM
Discovery	IBM—Tivoli Application Dependency Discovery Manager BMC Application Dependency Discovery Manager Microsoft System Center Configuration Manager HP Discovery and Dependency Mapping and HP Discovery and Dependency Mapping Inventory Flexera FlexNet Manager

Normalization	BDNA Data as a Service (DaaS) Flexera FlexNet Manager Aspera Smart Track
Metering	Microsoft System Center Configuration Manager
Release management	Part of IBM Smart Cloud Control Desk Part of CA Service Manager Part of HP Service Manager Part of ServiceNow ITSM Part of BMC Remedy ITSM
Change management	Part of IBM Smart Cloud Control Desk Part of CA Service Manager Part of HP Service Manager Part of ServiceNow ITSM Part of BMC Remedy ITSM
Deployment	SCCM Bladelogic
Security management	Multiple
Reconciliation and optimization	Flexera FlexNet Manager Aspera Smart Track
DSL	Any database Any network storage

11.1 Example of Tool Set for Solution

In most IT environments, you are likely to have more than one tool for the same functionality in the architecture because a single tool may not be good enough to deliver the desired outcome or because commercial reasons make more than one tool set viable. For example, ServiceNow discovery, which is a part of the ServiceNow platform and available with its ITSM product, is not good enough to meet the desired outcome, so you will need to supplement with additional tools. The following table gives such examples for two solutions discussed in this book.

Tool Function	**Holistic SAM Solution (see section 3)**		**Alternative Solution (see section 6)**
	Primary Tool	**Supporting Tool**	
Asset inventory tool	ServiceNow Discovery	BMC ADDM/ HP DDMA	IEM
Discovery tools	ServiceNow Discovery, MS SCCM	BMC ADDM/ HP DDMA	IEM/TADDM
Metering tool	Aspera	FlexNet	IEM SUA
License-management tool	Aspera	FlexNet	SCCD
Deployment management tools	Multiple	Multiple	IEM
Security tools	Multiple	Multiple	IEM
Reconciliation	Aspera	BDNA/FlexNet	SCCD
Asset Management workflow and repository	ServiceNow	ServiceNow	SCCD

12 APPENDIX 2: INDUSTRY ORGANIZATIONS

Organizations like ISACA and ITGA promote SAM practices from risk-management, service-management, and compliance perspectives; however, there are several industry organizations within the software licensing market focused at intellectual-property protection and raising the profile of software as an asset. A few prominent and well-known organizations are these:

BSA

BSA is the software alliance (http://www.bsa.org) for the global software industry before governments and was created to protect the interests of software manufactures and software creators. It was established in the United States and now has operations in more than sixty countries around the world. BSA has a strong compliance and enforcement agenda and promotes the legal use of software. The charter of BSA includes these elements:

1. **Compliance and enforcement:** Investigate software piracy and use lawsuits to prevent piracy.

2. **Enforcement:** Administer antipiracy enforcement program worldwide.
3. **Government relations and engagement:** Engage with governments to lobby for preventing software piracy.
4. **Compliance and enforcement communications:** Run worldwide antipiracy communications programs.
5. **Internet compliance and enforcement:** Track and prevent distribution of illegal software through Internet.
6. **Compliance tools:** Help the adoption of SAM tools.

SIIA

The Software & Information Industry Association (http://www.siia.net) is the organization formed by firms whose primary business is the creation of software, information, or other publishing, including distributors. It protects the business interests of member firms and industry with government relations, business development, corporate education, and intellectual-property protection. The mission of SIIA is the following:

1. Promote the interests of the software industry.
2. Protect the intellectual property of member companies.
3. Increase the awareness everywhere and communicate the contribution of the industry to the broader economy.

FAST

The Federation Against Software Theft (FAST) (http://www.fastiis.org) is a nonprofit organization to promote the legal use of software and to defend the intellectual-property rights of software publishers. FAST has been lobbying governments to bring forward legislation to increase the protection of intellectual property in software and to make it easier and less costly for authors to pursue their rights through the courts and was instrumental in changing the law to include software in the Copyright Act. FAST was also nicknamed the "software police" because of its antipiracy movements.

CCL

The Campaign for Clear Licensing (http://www.clearlicensing.org) is an independent, nonprofit organization campaigning for clear licensing, manageable license programs, and the rights of business software buyers. The mission of CCL is to reduce the indirect costs of using commercial software by improving the clarity and usability of software license terms and conditions.

CCL is the only organization that was founded to safeguard, protect, and promote software consumers' interests. The basic premise of CCL is that businesses are in agreement about the value of technology and are willing to pay a fair price for it. However, they are facing three key issues—namely, complex licensing, sharp sales practices, and threatening as well as aggressive audits. CCL is constantly campaigning for simplification of license complexity.

13 APPENDIX 3: ACRONYMS USED IN THE BOOK

AMC: Annual Maintenance Charges

BYOD: Bring Your Own Device

CCL: Campaign for Clear Licensing

CI: Configuration Item

CIO: Chief Information Officer

DSL: Definitive Software Library

ELP: effective License Position

FAST: Federation Against Software Theft

FSF: Free Software Foundation

GPL: General Public License

IaaS: Infrastructure As a Service

IEC: International Electrotechnical Commission

ISO: International Standard Organization

IT: Information Technology

ITAM: Information Technology Asset Management

ITIL: Information Technology Infrastructure Library

ITSM: Information Technology Service Management

LMDB: Landscape Management Database

M & A: Merger & Acquisition

MSP: Managed Service Provider

OCM: Organization Change Management

OEM: Original Equipment Manufacturer

OS: Operating System

PaaS: Platform As a Service

PVU: Processor value Unit

SAM: Software Asset Management

SDLC: Software Development Lifecycle

SIIA: Software & Information Industry Association

SLD: System Landscape Directory

T & C: Terms and Conditions

ABOUT THE AUTHORS

Prafull Verma

Prafull Verma has a bachelor's degree in electronics and communication engineering and has over thirty years' experience in the area of electronic data processing and information technology. He started his career in India in the area of electronic data processing systems and later moved to the United States in 1997. During the past thirty years, he has worked on diversified areas in computer science and information technologies. Some of his key experience areas are the design and implementation of heterogeneous networks, midrange technical support management, end-user service management and design, and the implementation and management of process-driven ITSM systems.

Prafull has acquired a unique blend of expertise in integrated areas of tools, process, governance, operations, and technology. He is the author of several methodology and frameworks for IT service management that include multi-vendor ITIL frameworks, ITSM for cloud computing and Service Integration.

Prafull's competencies and specializations include the area of merging engineering with service management, as this book manifests, and outsourcing business management.

Currently, Prafull is working for HCL Technologies Ltd., Infrastructure Service Division, and Cross Functional Service Business Unit, as chief ITSM architect. He is also serving member of the product advisory council of Service Now, the industry leading ITSM platform.

Kalyan Kumar

Kalyan Kumar (KK) is the Chief Technologist for HCL Technologies – ISD and leads all the Global Technology Practices.

In his current role Kalyan is responsible defining Architecture & Technology Strategy, New Solutions Development & Engineering across all Enterprise Infrastructure, Business Productivity, Unified Communication Collaboration & Enterprise Platform/DevOps Service Lines. Kalyan is also responsible for Business and Service Delivery for Cross Functional Services for HCL across all service lines globally.

Kalyan is widely acknowledged as an expert and path-breaker on BSM/ITSM & IT Architecture and Cloud Platforms and has developed many IPs for the company in these domains. He is also credited with building HCL MTaaS^{TM} Service from the scratch, which has a multi-million turnover today and a pro- prietary benchmark for Global IT Infrastructure Services Delivery. His team is also credited with developing the MyCloud^{SM} platform for Cloud Service Management & MyDevOps, which is a pioneering breakthrough in the Utility Computing and Hybrid Agile Ops Model space. He has been presented with many internal and industry awards for his thought leadership in the IT Management space.

Kalyan also runs the HCL ISD IPDEV Incubator Group where he is responsible for incubating new services, platforms and IPs for the company. He is also active in the Digital Systems Integration Roadmap and Solutions Strategy for HCL. He has also co-authored a Book **"Process excellence for IT Operations: A practical guide to IT service Management" (http://tinyurl .com/k7u3wyf)** and two more books are in pipeline of being published Kalyan has spoken at many prestigious industry platforms and is currently actively engaged in Partner Advisory Board of CA Technologies, IBM Software etc.

In his free time Kalyan likes to jam with his band Contraband as a drummer / percussionist and reviews Consumer Technology Gadgets and follows Cricket Games Diligently. Kalyan lives in New Delhi, India with his family.

KK can be followed on Twitter @KKLIVE and at Linkedin (http://www. linkedin. com/in/kalyankumar).

FROM THE SAME AUTHORS

Process Excellence for IT Operations: a Practical Guide for IT Service Process Management

Authored by Mr Prafull Verma, Authored by Mr Kalyan Kumar B

List Price: **$29.95**
6" x 9" (15.24 x 22.86 cm)
Black & White on White paper
332 pages
Process Excellence for IT Operations
ISBN-13: 978-0615877525 (Custom Universal)
ISBN-10: 0615877524
BISAC: Computers / Information Technology

As the title suggests, the book is providing a practical guidance on managing the processes for IT Services. There are lot of guidance available on technology management in IT industry but this book is focusing on technology independent service management. The book will be addressed to all IT people from a process practitioner perspective, however, the fundamentals are presented in simplistic terms, and therefore it should be useful to all IT people. It will describe the process engineering concept and how it can be applied to IT Service Management. This is not about the industry standard framework such as ITIL and COBIT but about the common processes that are generally used in real life operations. This book does not focus on any technology.

Foundation of IT Operations Management: Event Monitoring and Controls

Authored by Mr. Prafull Verma, Authored by Mr. Kalyan Kumar

List Price: **$15.95**
6" x 9" (15.24 x 22.86 cm)
Black & White on White paper
138 pages
Foundation Of IT Operation
ISBN-13: 978-0692205709 (Custom Universal)
ISBN-10: 0692205705
BISAC: Computers / Information Technology

In IT operations, event monitoring and control - where you continuously monitor the health of IT infrastructure and take proactive measures to prevent the interruptions in IT services- is dominated by tools and technology but there is a meticulous process behind it. This book tries to demystify the underlying process for this kind of operation management. There are lot many books on service management but those books do not cover this subject adequately and leave this area to be addressed by tools and technology. Tools vendor on the other hand, focus on the tool part, leaving the process aspect to the service management professionals. This book fills in the void and connects both, the process and the tools to provide a holistic view. The book takes an educative tone and written primarily for IT generalist and not for the tool experts, although it would give a new perspective to tool experts also.

Service Integration: A Practical Guide to Multivendor Service Management

Authored by Prafull Verma, Authored by Kalyan Kumar

List Price: **$15.95**
5.5" x 8.5" (13.97 x 21.59 cm)
Black & White on White paper
148 pages
Service Integration
ISBN-13: 978-0692219959 (Custom Universal)
ISBN-10: 0692219951
BISAC: Computers / Information Technology

This book is intended to present simplified guide for IT generalists who are new to the service integration subject. The purpose of this book is to educate all IT professionals with the basic concepts of the service integration. Additionally the purpose is to provide the core guidance and foundation guidance to Service Management professionals, upon which they can build and implement the service integration in their environment.